CITYSPOTS
ROME

Thomas

OST PAVLVS·V·BVRGHESIVS·ROMANVS·PON

Written by Zoë Ross with assistance from Frances Folsom
Updated by Giovanna Dunmall

Published by Thomas Cook Publishing
A division of Thomas Cook Tour Operations Limited
Company registration No: 1450464 England
The Thomas Cook Business Park, 9 Coningsby Road
Peterborough PE3 8SB, United Kingdom
Email: books@thomascook.com, Tel: +44 (0)1733 416477
www.thomascookpublishing.com

Produced by The Content Works Ltd
Aston Court, Kingsmead Business Park, Frederick Place
High Wycombe, Bucks HP11 1LA
www.thecontentworks.com

Series design based on an original concept by Studio 183 Limited

ISBN: 978-1-84848-046-9

First edition © 2007 Thomas Cook Publishing
This second edition © 2009 Thomas Cook Publishing
Text © Thomas Cook Publishing
Maps © Thomas Cook Publishing/PCGraphics (UK) Limited
Transport map © Communicarta Limited

Project Editor: Adam Royal
Production/DTP: Steven Collins

Printed and bound in Spain by GraphyCems

Cover photography (St Peter's Basilica) © Thomas Cook

CONTENTS

CITYSPOTS

SYMBOLS KEY

The following symbols are used throughout this book:

ⓐ address ⓣ telephone ⓕ fax ⓦ website address
ⓛ opening times ⓝ public transport connections ⓘ important

The following symbols are used on the maps:

𝒊	information office	▪	points of interest
✈	airport	○	city
✚	hospital	○	large town
🛡	police station	○	small town
🚍	bus station	═	motorway
🚆	railway station	—	main road
Ⓜ	metro	—	minor road
✝	cathedral	—	railway
❶	numbers denote featured cafés & restaurants

Hotels and restaurants are graded by approximate price as follows:
£ budget price ££ mid-range price £££ expensive

◗ St Peter's Basilica dominates Rome's skyline

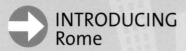

Introduction

Few other cities in the world have such a wealth of historic beauty,
preserving the wonders of one of the most fascinating ancient
civilisations – hence its nickname, *la Città Eterna* ('Eternal City'). For
21st-century visitors, these historic treasures can now be admired
in even greater glory, after a large majority of the monuments and
statues were restored as part of the Millennium projects in 2000.
By day, they draw you in like a living and breathing history book,
as you imagine the ancient footsteps that once trod the path you
now tread; by night, the artfully placed floodlights create a magical
glow of a timeless fairyland.

Italy may not have been fully united and Rome declared its
capital until 1870, but with its central position the city has always
been integral to this boot-shaped landscape. The one-time political
centre of one of the world's most successful and important empires
and the nucleus of the Christian church since the reported arrival
of St Peter in the first century AD, Rome's influence has never been
disputed. But, as with many capital cities, it is often looked on with
disdain by the rest of the country. Romans are generally considered
to be lazy and somewhat rude, compared to, say, the cultured
refinement of the Florentines or the Bolognese. Romans, however,
would argue that, as citizens of this bustling and important
metropolis, they have less time for the niceties of daily life.

None of this, however, should influence the visitor to one of
Europe's most enchanting cities. You don't even have to be a history
buff to marvel at all there is to offer – imagining the roar of the
crowd in the Colosseum, the ancient trading cries in the Forum, the
wealthy lifestyles in the Renaissance *palazzi*, as well as the modern-
day hum of the ubiquitous Vespas still embracing *la dolce vita*.

An important thing to remember, however, is that in a city so rich in heritage you cannot possibly see it all in one visit. Even a month here would allow you only to experience the basics, and the Vatican City alone warrants several days' exploration. For the first-time visitor, focus on a few of the unmissables, then give sightseeing a break, sit back and relax. History aside, one of the greatest charms of Rome is an early evening drink in the Piazza Navona, or a stroll through the alleyways in Trastevere, strung with laundry overhead. *This* is Rome today, and it's as vibrant as it has always been.

◔ *Experience Rome's long history at the Colosseum*

When to go

There are no hard and fast rules about when you should visit
Rome – year round it has something to offer any visitor. However,
July and August can be uncomfortably hot (see below), and the
latter month sees an exodus of locals: you might have more space
in which to discover the city, but you'll also be relatively hard
pressed to find somewhere to have lunch or buy your postcards!
All in all, spring and autumn are better times to visit (although
avoid Easter, unless you want to share the city with heaving masses)
as the weather then is generally dry, warm and sunny. Winter, too,
has its advantages in that you'll have far fewer queues to get into
the attractions.

Whenever you visit, you must bring the right togs. Comfortable,
hard-wearing shoes are required. The easiest way to get from one
sight to another is usually on foot, but pavement and floor surfaces
are generally uneven. Even in places such as the Vatican Museums,
you will be covering vast distances. In summer, cotton and linen
clothing will be the coolest options, but don't forget a jacket or
shawl. Not only do the evenings get cool, but underground sights
such as catacombs can be alarmingly chilly compared to the
baking sun outside.

SEASONS & CLIMATE

In the height of summer, the city can get more than a little
warm. Temperatures in excess of 35°C (95°F) are not unknown,
and the heat can combine with humidity to make things a touch
unpleasant. Spring and autumn are usually lovely and, apart from
very occasional days that see a sprinkling of snow, winters are not
particularly cold.

ANNUAL EVENTS

Romans love to party, and whether it's a national holiday, the start of another arts or music extravaganza, or simply an obscure saint's day, the chances are you'll come across some kind of *festa* (festival) or another. Furthermore, any holiday that falls midweek is an invitation to *fare il ponte* (literally 'do a bridge'), which means that an extra day or two before the weekend are also holidays. What follows are just a few of the hundreds of special events and festivals celebrated in the city throughout the year.

January
Epifania (Feast of the Epiphany) A day on which La Befana, a witch, is said to reward good children with presents. 🕐 6 Jan

February–March
Carnevale The last fling before Lent. Children dress up in costumes, and parades are held around the city.

March–April
Settimana Santa & Pasqua (Holy Week & Easter) Tourists and pilgrims pour into Rome on the Saturday before Palm Sunday, filling St Peter's Square (Piazza San Pietro) for the open-air Mass. Holy Week brings numerous religious services, culminating with the Papal Address on Easter Sunday. On Pasquetta (Easter Monday), by tradition Romans *fuori porta* (head for the mountains and parks outside the city) to relax and feast on picnics of *uove sode* (hard-boiled eggs) and *salumi* (cured meats). 🔊 Vatican: Bus: 23, 40, 62, 64, 115, 116, 271, 280

Settimana dei Beni Culturali (Cultural Heritage Week) All state-owned museums and the many fascinating archaeological sites throughout

⬤ *Many festivals are held in Rome's historical buildings*

Rome are open to the public free of charge. ❶ 39 066 7231
🕐 First week in April

June–September
Estate Romana In addition to the innumerable independently
run arts festivals that cram the summer calendar, there are many
city-run cultural events under the banner of *Estate Romana* (Roman
Summer). For three months open-air concerts, plays and ballet
performances are staged in venues dotted around the city. Many
of the Estate Romana events are free: check newspapers, online and
tourist boards for details. 🌐 www.estateromana.comune.roma.it

September–November

RomaEuropa Festival Following on, almost indistinguishably, from *Estate Romana*, is this autumn arts festival of music, dance and theatre. Buy tickets at the venues, online or by phone.
Ⓦ www.romaeuropa.net

December

Immacolata Concezione (Feast of the Immaculate Conception)
A member of the local fire brigade, overseen by the Pope, is raised on a hydraulic platform to lay a wreath at the feet of the statue of Madonna (which stands on top of a great stone column in the Piazza di Spagna). 🕘 8 Dec

---

PUBLIC HOLIDAYS

Capodanno (New Year's Day) 1 Jan

Epifania (Epiphany) 6 Jan

Pasqua (Easter Sunday) 12 Apr 2009; 4 Apr 2010; 24 Apr 2011

Lunedi di Pasqua (Easter Monday) 13 Apr 2009; 5 Apr 2010; 25 Apr 2011

Festa della Liberazione (Liberation Day) 25 Apr

Festa del Lavoro (Labour Day) 1 May

Festa della Repubblica (Anniversary of the Republic) 2 June

Ferragosto (Feast of the Assumption) 15 Aug

Tutti Santi (All Saints' Day) 1 Nov

Immacolata Concezione (Feast of the Immaculate Conception) 8 Dec

Natale (Christmas) 25 Dec

St Stephen's Day 26 Dec

Easter

As the centre of the Roman Catholic church the two weeks leading up to Easter are the busiest time of the year in Rome. Tens of thousands of pilgrims and tourists who just want to enjoy the spectacle flood the city, taking up every hotel room in the place.

Tickets for the Masses and events are free but need to be reserved in advance. Check the Vatican website (ⓦ www.vatican.va) for details and ticketing information. It's possible to attend without a ticket, but you'll have to stand for long periods of time.

Maundy/Holy Thursday – morning

At a special Mass (the Chrismal Mass), held in St Peter's Basilica (Basilica di San Pietro, see page 98) at 09.30, the Pope blesses the holy oils. This is one of the best times to get a glimpse of the Pope.

● *Thousands come to hear the Pope's Address at St Peter's Basilica*

Maundy/Holy Thursday – evening

The Triduum (three-day period between Holy Thursday and Easter Sunday) officially begins with the Pope holding a Mass at 17.30 in the **Basilica di San Giovanni in Laterano** (❷ Piazza San Giovanni in Laterano 4) to commemorate the Last Supper.

Good Friday – afternoon

Mass is said in the Vatican Chapel of St Peter's at 17.00, during which St John's account of Christ's suffering and death (known as 'the Passion') is sung and all present may kiss the cross.

Good Friday – evening

Starting at 21.15, the Pope leads a solemn torch-lit procession, the *Via Crucis* (Ways of the Cross), from the Colosseum (see page 92) to Palatine Hill, re-enacting the 14 Stations of the Cross from Jesus' death sentence to the placement of his body in the tomb. Like his predecessors, the Pope carries a large wooden cross and at every station stops and offers a brief prayer. At the final station he gives his liturgy.

Holy Saturday

At 21.00, in the Papal Chapel of St Peter's, the Pope conducts the Easter Vigil, commencing the five-week Easter season.

Easter Sunday

The Pope celebrates Mass in St Peter's Square (see page 98) before delivering the *Urbi et Orbi* (meaning 'blessings on the city and the world') benediction from the Central Loggia of St Peter's Basilica.

History

The most popular legend surrounding the foundation of Rome, but undoubtedly pure myth, is that it was established by the twin brothers Romulus and Remus. The product of a rape by Mars of a Vestal Virgin, the young twins were cast aside and left to fend for themselves until they were rescued by a she-wolf who nursed them into adulthood. As adults, however, they became rival leaders of the city they created in what is now the Palatine Hill area and Remus was eventually murdered by Romulus. The latter therefore gave the city its name and became the first of its seven kings in 753 BC.

Nobody knows where this legend originated, but in reality it was the Etruscans who established the city, as they did much of Italy, in the eight or ninth century BC. The Palatine and Capitoline hills were a strategic choice for its foundation, protected by the lofty location while also being able to utilise the water source of the River Tiber. Proof of their existence here has emerged in various guises – ninth-century BC huts have been excavated beneath Palatine Hill, while historical documents tell tales of an Etruscan king in the region, Tarquinius Priscus, who reigned from 616 BC.

Documents also show that in 509 BC the son of King Tarquinius raped Lucretia, the wife of Collatinus, a Roman. Traumatised by the event, Lucretia committed suicide, but not before craftily telling her husband and his friend Brutus what had happened. In anger, grief and vengeance Collatinus and Brutus led a rebellion against the Tarquins, overthrowing the Etruscan dynasty and eventually establishing the Roman Republic. It was not just the city that grew in size and wealth; over the ensuing centuries the Romans proved themselves successful in expelling all other tribes, including the Sabines and the Samnites, as well as the Etruscans. Then, not content with a countrywide republic, they cast their sights further afield, eventually governing much of western Europe under the banner of the Roman Empire.

The secret of their success is manifold. They were superb military leaders (with Julius Caesar among the finest), and understood the importance of establishing cities wherever they conquered to ensure continued control. They were also great politicians and masters of construction. The Via Appia (Appian Way), begun in 312 BC, not only linked Rome with southern Italy, and thereby Greece, but also became the prototype for all future Roman roads. At the same time, the Aqua Appia was the first aqueduct, illustrating how to bring fresh water from the river to the city. The construction of ports allowed trade links to grow and prosper, while the concept of a central forum established a link between traders, citizens and leaders.

It couldn't last, however. When Emperor Constantine converted to Christianity and moved the empire's capital to Byzantium, Rome became susceptible to invading tribes such as the Goths and the Vandals and by AD 476 the empire had fallen.

That was then. These days, Rome's glory is of a somewhat different nature, but it's no less impressive: now it springs from the city's countless attractions and from its status as not only Europe's most glamorous European capital but also the world centre of stylish living.

In May 2008 the city elected a new mayor, Gianni Alemanno. Alemanno has promised to sharpen the focus of both the city and its citizens on increasing the already massive amount of money that's brought in by tourism. *La vita* in Rome is about to get even more *dolce*.

Lifestyle

Elegant and suave, sipping coffee in outdoor cafés or lounging around on their scooters, Romans deeply love their city and city life. That love is not blind, however, and while they can wax lyrical about its historical, cultural and architectural wonders, they also lament its traffic congestion, high pollution levels (which have improved), high cost of living, demonstrators regularly blocking city squares, disruptions caused by the high security for visiting VIPs, wildcat transport strikes that bring the city to a grinding halt, roadworks and bumper-to-bumper tour buses to name a few.

That said, ask a Roman if they would want to live anywhere else and they will look at you as if you have two heads.

The pace of life may be frantic, but there's never a dull moment. To an extent, clichéd images hold true: nuns dodge the traffic alongside mobile phone-toting businessmen, clad in Armani and sporting slicked back hair. Impossibly handsome teenagers flirt with each other in market squares such as Campo de' Fiori, while considerably stouter *mammas* stock up on fresh fruit and veg. Expat writers and artists while away the afternoon at a café in Piazza Navona while in nearby alleyways local *ragazzi* try to find room to kick about their beloved footballs. This is a city that welcomes one and all.

The city centre may appear to be almost entirely inhabited by tourists and their ubiquitous cameras – and to a large extent it is. But there are many other layers to Rome, found in the lesser-known districts. The city changes constantly. Testaccio has become a trendy place to live, and upmarket cafés, *trattorie* and wine bars have sprung up in recent years. The gritty and formerly industrial area of Ostiense has also become home to many restaurants and a pulsating nightlife scene.

In recent years Rome has had a reputation as a gay and lesbian centre. However, remember that this is a very Catholic city, and male *machismo* is rife. Same-sex couples should avoid public displays of affection. Gay/lesbian organisations in Rome are: **Arcigay Roma ORA** (ⓦ www.arcigay.it/roma), **Circolo Mario Mieli** (ⓦ www.mariomieli.org), **Di Gay Project** (ⓦ www.digayproject.org) and **Epicentro Ursino Romano** (ⓦ www.epicentroursino.com).

⬥ *Wander along the Ponte Sisto over the River Tiber*

Culture

Rome's one and only official arts centre, the **Palazzo delle Esposizioni** (⊜ Via Nazionale 194 ⓦ www.palaexpo.it), was built in the 19th century specifically to host art exhibitions, a role it still fulfils. Exhibitions are held on three floors, and there's a cinema, book shop, café and restaurant.

Major art exhibits have a spectacular venue in the **Scuderie del Quirinal** (⊜ Via XXIV Maggio 16 ⓣ 06 69 62 70 ⓦ www.scuderiequirinal.it), the former stables of the Palazzo Pontifico sul Quirinale. Built in 1730, the building has been beautifully renovated by the Italian architect Gae Aulenti (of Paris's Musée d'Orsay fame). The Scuderie houses impressive works of art by 17th- and 18th-century master painters, as well as touring exhibitions.

For a slightly more avant-garde cultural experience, check out the Centri Sociali, non-profit, self-governing social centres set up in various disused buildings around the city. They're a tradition begun by left-wing students during the 1970s, and still stage off-the-wall concerts, plays, arthouse film screenings and much more. It's a youthful scene – places where the under-30s can come for a drink, a political debate, a simple meal and some hard-hitting entertainment, although some resemble little more than a glorified squat. If this is your thing, the daily newspaper *La Repubblica* will give details of event times and places.

A relatively recent addition to Rome's cultural scene is the **Parco della Musica** (⊜ Viale Pietro de Coubertin ⓣ 06 802 41281 ⓦ www.auditorium.com), designed by Renzo Piano and opened in 2002. Its three concert halls of varying size as well as an outdoor

---

▶ *Enjoy an opera or ballet at the popular Teatro dell'Opera*

amphitheatre have played host to a vast and distinguished list of performers as well as numerous greats of the classical scene.

Although not on the scale of Milan's La Scala, the **Teatro dell'Opera di Roma** (ⓐ Via Beniamino 1 ① 06 481 60287 Ⓦ www.operaroma.it) has stellar performances by Rome's opera and ballet companies. The season runs from October to June.

Opera has also returned to the **Baths of Caracalla** (ⓐ Piazza Beniamino Gigli ① 06 481 60255 Ⓦ www.operaroma.it) as part of the Teatro dell'Opera di Roma programme. The largest thermal baths in the world date from the third century and were in use until the fall of the Roman Empire. The idea of staging opera here belonged to Mussolini, but by 1993 productions were shut down because the 5,000-strong audiences were damaging the ruins. Restoration work was undertaken, audience size was reduced to 2,000 and opera recommenced here in 2000. The season is short – early July to mid-August – so reserve early.

Throughout summer, open-air performances are held in parks and archaeological sites. Information can be found at tourist offices and in local newspapers. See Ⓦ www.inromenow.com and Ⓦ www.2night.it for details, too.

● *Millions visit St Peter's Basilica every year*

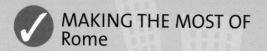

MAKING THE MOST OF
Rome

Shopping

Rome may be a bustling and hectic city, but shopping here is still remarkably quite a personalised experience. A lot of the streets are pedestrianised, which means you can window shop at leisure without keeping one eye out for traffic, and there is a wide range of markets that offer an authentic Italian experience. Rome has also retained a strong tradition of craftsmanship and there are many skilled artisans who take great pride in their work.

Most shops in the centre of Rome stay open all day. However, many, particularly in the outer districts, still observe traditional Italian hours: 15.30–19.30 Mon, 09.30–13.30, 15.30–19.30 Tues–Sat, closed on Sun. Food shops are often closed on Saturday afternoons in summer and Thursday afternoons in winter. Many shops close for at least two weeks between mid-July and mid-September.

The streets close to the Spanish Steps – Via Condotti, Via Borgognona and Via Frattina – are the ones to head for if you're after true Italian designer style, and designer prices. Here you'll find household names such as Gucci, Prada, Valentino, Bulgari, Versace and Armani. For those with a slightly lighter wallet, head to Via del Tritone, Via Nazionale, below Piazza della Repubblica, or Via Cola di Rienzo near the Vatican, where you'll still find plenty of style but with a more realistic price tag. The shops on and around Via del Corso will keep any teenager happy, while Via dei Giubbonari offers chic boutiques and hip designers. Via del Governo Vecchio offers a density of local fashion names.

If you're in the mood for antiques shopping, whether it be Renaissance furniture or retro 1960s Bakelite, head for Via dei Coronari, Via del' Orso and Via dei Soldati, north of Piazza Navona. Another good source of art and antiques is Via Giulia and the area between

Piazza del Popolo and the Spanish Steps. The largest flea market in Rome – and, some say, in Europe – is held every Sunday in Trastevere.

Rome abounds in food shops, but the best option is the markets around Campo de' Fiori or Via Cola di Rienzo across the river. These are always worth a visit for sheer street theatre.

USEFUL SHOPPING PHRASES

What time do the shops open/close?
A che ora aprono/chiudono i negozi?
Ah keh ohrah ahprohnoh/kewdohnoh ee nehgotsee?

How much is this?
Quanto costa questo?
Kwantoh kostah kwestoh?

Can I try this on?
Posso provarlo?
Pohsoh prohvarloh?

My size is …
La mia taglia è …
Lah meeyah tahlyah eh …

I'll take this one, thank you
Prenderò questo, grazie
Prehndehroh kwestoh, grahtsyeh

Can you show me the one in the window/this one?
Può mostrarmi quello in vetrina/questo?
Poh mohstrahrmee kwehloh een vehtreenah/kwestoh?

This is too large/too small/too expensive
Questo è troppo grande/troppo piccolo/troppo caro
Kwestoh eh trohpoh grahndeh/ trohpoh peekohloh/ trohpoh kahroh

Eating & drinking

Italians as a whole are in love with food, so it's no surprise that the capital would also place cuisine very high on its agenda. In even the most modest of establishments, your food is likely to be the freshest that is available that day – Italians hold little sway with frozen meat or vegetables. Their insistence on quality is also shown by the amount of time they like to spend savouring the produce – even busy Romans will take hours out of their day to spend them eating and socialising over lunch or dinner.

In recent years the restaurant scene in Rome has also gone up a notch. As well as traditional *trattorie*, serving simple pasta and meat dishes, there are now trendy mozzarella bars, wine bars serving gourmet dishes and so-called *ristodisco*, places where you can both eat and dance. Even the humble pizza has been given a new lease of life.

If you're not a fan of Italian cuisine, however, you're likely to go hungry. Italy, and by the same token Rome, is so proud of its own creations that it's never really felt the need to embrace other cultures on this front. There are, however, a few decent Chinese, Japanese and Indian restaurants.

One speciality in Rome that may not appeal to all tastes is the use of animal offal – the *quinto quarto*, or 'fifth quarter' parts of

PRICE CATEGORIES

The restaurant price guides used in the book indicate the approximate cost of a three-course meal for one person, excluding drinks, at the time of writing.

£ up to €25   ££ €25–50   £££ over €50

○ *Watch the world go by over a drink in Piazza di Pietra*

a beast that are left over after the prime cuts of meat are sold off. That means *cervello* (brains), *nervetti* (beef tendons), *coda* (oxtail), *pajata* (baby veal intestines) and *animelle* (the thymus glands in an animal's throat) can often be seen on menus. *Trattorie* in the neighbourhoods of Testaccio and Trastevere are known for these delicacies.

Vegetarians should have no problem in choosing a suitable option from any menu. Many pasta dishes and pizzas are made entirely without meat, and lentils and other pulses are a frequent

offering. Fresh vegetables and cheeses are also plentiful.

Restaurants are generally open from 12.30–16.00, then again from 19.30–00.00, and some stay open later. A few are open through the day.

❶ Remember many places are closed in August. It's also a good idea to make reservations in advance, particularly in high season, and at the weekend, when it's busier.

🔻 *Linger at one of Rome's many al fresco restaurants*

The typical Italian meal starts with *antipasti*, which are tapas-style bitesize variations of cold cuts, seafood and vegetables. Next, *Il Primo* (first course) is usually a soup or pasta dish, followed by *Il Secondo* (second course), consisting of meat or fish. Italians rarely eat pasta as a main course, so portions are smaller than you would find in Italian restaurants abroad. Vegetables (*contorni*) are ordered separately, so don't assume your main course will come with an accompaniment unless you order them. The meal usually ends

USEFUL DINING PHRASES

I would like a table for ... people
Vorrei un tavolo per ... persone
Vohray oon tahvohloh pehr... pehrsohneh

Excuse me!
Scusi!
Skoozhee!

May I have the bill, please?
Mi dà il conto, per favore?
Mee dah eel cohntoh pehr fahvohreh?

Could I have it well-cooked/medium/rare please?
Potrei averlo ben cotto/mediamente cotto/ al sangue, per favore?
Pohtray ahvehrloh behn kohtoh/ mehdyahmehnteh kohtoh/ ahl sahngweh, pehr fahvohreh?

I am a vegetarian. Does this contain meat?
Sono vegetariano/vegetariana (fem.). Contiene carne?
Sohnoh vehjehtehrehahnoh/vehjehtehrehahnah. Kontyehneh kahrneh?

TIPPING

A service charge of 10–15 per cent will often be included, in which case no further tip is required. Restaurants are no longer allowed to add the *pane e coperto* (bread and cover charge) to the bill. However, some establishments blithely ignore this and charge it anyway. A tip of between five and ten percent of the bill is always adequate.

with *frutta* (fresh fruit) and a selection of *dolci* (sweet desserts), followed by coffee and a *digestivo* (liqueur). Five courses may seem like a lot, but remember that portion sizes reflect this, and no one will frown on you if you order less, as many now do. Few restaurants impose a strict dress code, although shorts and t-shirts are frowned upon in the more exclusive places.

Ask for *il conto* when you want the bill – but expect a bit of a wait. Romans are never in a hurry to leave the dining table and waiters are used to this attitude.

Children are welcome in Roman restaurants, even the posh ones. Usually *un seggiolone* (a high-chair) is available on request, as is *una mezza porzione* (a half portion).

Many of Rome's clubs are trendy places where the 'beautiful people' go to see and be seen. The *enoteca* or *vineria* (wine bar) has always been a favourite hang-out in Rome. Most of them, particularly the newer ones, offer extensive wine lists and gourmet menus.

ⓘ Smoking is now illegal in all restaurants and bars, except outdoors.

Entertainment & nightlife

Everything you've ever thought about Italian style and posing becomes apparent when you walk through the door of Rome's more popular clubs. If you want cheaper prices and less fashion pressure, however, head for the smaller venues – you'll find details in local listings magazines. To beat the licensing laws, many of Rome's clubs are listed as private, which means they charge a membership fee just to enter, although this usually includes the price of a drink.

The best areas for nightlife can be found in Trastevere, the Centro Storico (around Piazza Navona in particular), Testaccio and Ostiense (to the southwest of Trastevere). Pick up a copy of *Roma C'e* (ⓦ www.romace.it), published every Wednesday and available from newsagents (approximately €1) which has a section in English. Otherwise *TrovaRoma*, in *La Repubblica*'s Thursday edition, is another helpful guide. The fortnightly English-language *Wanted in Rome* magazine (ⓦ www.wantedinrome.com) lists events.

City-wide venues feature summer festivals of live music; mid-June through to September welcomes the Jazz & Image Festival at the Villa Celimontana park. October brings the **Roma Jazz Festival** (ⓦ www.romajazz.com), which attracts big-name musicians.

Latin music is gaining in popularity, so if you fancy a bit of salsa beat don't miss **Fiesta!** (ⓦ www.fiesta.it). The festival runs from mid-June to mid-August at **Ippodromo delle Campannelle** (ⓐ Via Appia Nuova).

Other live music offerings in summer include the **Luglio suona bene** (ⓦ www.auditorium.com/lugliosuonabene) programme of jazz, pop and rock concerts (with international headliners) that takes place throughout the month of July in Parco della Musica (see page 18). The **Cosmophonies** music festival (ⓦ www.cosmophonies.com) hosts grand concerts in the amphitheatre of Ostia Antica (see page 119). Roma Incontra Il Mondo, a series of concerts with Italian and world music performers, takes place every year from late June to mid-August against the atmospheric backdrop of the **Villa Ada** park (Ⓦ www.villaada.org and Ⓦ www.estateromana.comune.roma.it).

🔺 *Romantic Rome by night*

Sport & relaxation

Rome was, of course, home to the crowd-jeering gladiatorial fights in ancient times, so it has a long tradition of providing spectator sports. The national sport, in fact obsession, is *calcio* (football) and during big matches you'll see most Romans glued to the small screen in bars and cafés. On the whole, sport is seen very much as something to watch rather than do – but these days there are more *palestre* (gyms) in town than ever before.

PARTICIPATION SPORTS
Cycling
The month of May brings the *Giro d'Italia* (Italy's national race), when competitive cyclists can be seen spinning through Rome's narrow cobbled streets. At any other time of the year, Rome's incessant traffic makes cycling a death-wish choice, but on Sundays the Via Appia Antica is closed to automobiles, offering the chance to get on two wheels for a leisurely afternoon; there's a bike hire outlet at the information point on Via Appia Antica (🕒 09.30–13.30, 14.00–17.30 Mon–Sat).

SPECTATOR SPORTS
Football
Rome has two principal football teams, Roma and Lazio, both of which play at the **Stadio Olimpico** (🅐 Via Foro Italico, off Via della Stadio Olimpico 🕿 06 323 7333) on alternate Sundays from September to May. As a rule, Roma is the favourite of the left-wing working class while Lazio is the team of choice for the conservative populace. Rivalries run high and the sport can be quite violent, on and off the playing field. Stadio Olimpico seats around 82,000 for most games.

With the exception of Roma–Lazio clashes, tickets should be available on the day of the event.

Lazio supporters sit on the *Curva Nord* (North end) of the stadium waving their colours of blue and white, with the eagle as their symbol. Roma fans, whose symbol is the wolf and whose colours are blue and yellow, take over the *Curva Sud* (South end) of the stadium. If you attend a game make sure you're cheering for the right team on the right side if you want to avoid any trouble.

For information in English about the season's games, go to the *Federazione Italiana Giuoco Calcio* (Ⓦ www.figc.it). Or if you read Italian, pick up the Rome paper *Corriere dello Sport*, which gives details of upcoming games.

Ticket prices vary from €15–€100. They can be purchased at special kiosks or lotto outlets throughout Rome, at the box office on the day of the game, or at the Roma-Lazio clubs. See Ⓦ www.asroma.it and Ⓦ www.sslazio.it for details of how to obtain them.

⬤ *Fans prepare for a match at the Stadio Olimpico*

Accommodation

Rome has a vast range of hotel accommodation so even if you arrive in the city without a booking you're likely to be able to find a room. However, if you're travelling in high season (Easter to October and Christmas to New Year) it's best to book in advance, as it would be anywhere else.

If you want to find a room on arrival your best bets are the Enjoy Rome office (see page 153) or the **Free Hotel Reservation Service** (**☎** 06 505 12610 **w** www.freereservation.com), where multilingual staff will search out hotels for you.

HOTELS

Aphrodite £–££ This government-rated 3-star hotel, located next to Termini Station, not only offers comfortable en suite rooms but also benefits from a roof terrace, which is a godsend in the summer. Female travellers in particular, however, should take care in the area at night. **a** Via Marsala 90 (Piazza Venezia & Capitoline Hill) **☎** 06 49 10 96 **w** www.aphroditehotelrome.com **Ⓜ** Metro: Termini

Arenula £–££ Set in a charming 19th-century building, all the rooms benefit from private baths, television and telephone. Those with restricted mobility should ask for lower floor rooms, as there's no lift.

PRICE CATEGORIES
The ratings in this book are for a double room for one night (excluding VAT and breakfast).
£ up to €100   **££** €100–200   **£££** over €200

ⓐ Via S Maria de'Calderari 47 (Centro Storico) ⓘ 06 687 9454
ⓦ www.hotelarenula.com Ⓝ Bus: 30, 40, 46, 62, 64, 70, 81, 87, 119, 186,
190, 492, 571, 628, 810, 916; Tram: 8

Cervia £–££ A wonderful-value *pensione* given its location right in
the city centre. All rooms have private baths. The top floor rooms
are cheaper because there's no lift. ⓐ Via Palestro 55 (Piazza Venezia
& Capitoline Hill) ⓘ 06 49 10 57 ⓦ www.hotelcerviaroma.com Ⓝ Bus:
16, 36, 75, 90, 92, 204, 217, 310, 360, 492, 649; Metro: Castro Pretoria

Gerber £–££ Comfortable and clean and very conveniently situated
between Villa Borghese and St Peter's, ideal for sightseeing. Rates
include breakfast and taxes. ⓐ Via degli Scipioni 241 (Vatican City)
ⓘ 06 321 6485 ⓦ www.hotelgerber.it Ⓝ Bus: 30, 70, 130, 186, 224, 280,
590, 913; Metro: Lepanto

Daphne Inns ££ These two boutique hotels offer great value for
money, particularly given their situation – one near the Trevi Fountain,
the other off Via Veneto. Each room has been decorated to a high
standard, although not all are en suite. Breakfast is included.
Daphne Trevi: Rooms are on the second and third floors, no lift.
Some shared baths. ⓐ Via degli Avignonesi 20 (Piazza Venezia
& Capitoline Hill)
Daphne Veneto: All rooms have private baths. There is a lift. ⓐ Via
di San Basilio 55 (Piazza Venezia & Capitoline Hill) ⓘ 06 874 50086
ⓦ www.daphne-rome.com Ⓝ Bus: 52, 53, 61, 62, 63, 80, 95, 116, 119, 175,
492, 630; Metro: Barberini

Isa ££ This boutique hotel is in the elegant Prati district, between
the Vatican and the Spanish Steps. All rooms are en suite and

breakfast is included. @ Via Cicerone 39 (Vatican City) ☎ 06 661 63224
ⓦ www.boutiquehotelisa.com ⓥ Bus: 30, 70, 186, 280, 590, 913;
Metro: Lepanto

🔺 The elegant Isa Hotel has a great location

Aleph £££ A boutique hotel with a glamorous lobby, a buzzing bar and restaurant, bedrooms with 1930s- and 40s-inspired furniture, and a beautiful spa with a mosaic whirlpool downstairs. ❸ Via San Basilio 15 (Vatican City) ❶ 06 42 29 01 ⓦ www.boscolohotels.com ⓝ Bus: 61, 62, 116, 150, 175, 492, 590; Metro: Barberini

Portrait Suites £££ This apartment-style boutique hotel in Rome's high-fashion neighbourhood is a sophisticated outpost of the Salvatore Ferragamo fashion empire. The rooftop terrace alone is worth the money; it offers one of the most sumptuous views of the city. ❸ Via Bocca de Leone 23 (Ancient Rome) ❶ 06 693 80742 ⓦ www.lungarnohotels.com ⓝ Bus: 116, 117, 119, 590; Metro: Spagna

St George Roma £££ The St George is a great little contemporary hotel right in the heart of Rome, on a beautiful, quiet cobbled street a short walk away from the bustling Campo de' Fiori and St Peter's. There's a spa and restaurant, too. ❸ Via Giulia 62 (Centro Storico) ❶ 06 68 66 11 ⓦ www.stgeorgehotel.it ⓝ Bus: 23, 40, 46, 64, 116, 271, 280, 571, 916

HOSTELS
Alessandro Palace Hostels £ These two hostels have been voted among the top ten in Europe, so understandably they're always crowded. Book in advance. The Alessandro Palace (below) has en suite baths in every room, unusual for hostel accommodation, while the Downtown Alessandro (opposite) has dormitory rooms and shared baths. Amenities at both include breakfast, internet access, free soft drinks and free weekly pizza parties. Both are a ten-minute walk from Termini Station.
Alessandro Palace Hostel ❸ Via Vicenza 42 (Piazza Venezia &

Capitoline Hill) ☎ 06 446 1958 ⓦ www.hostelalessandropalace.com
ⓝ Metro: Termini Station, exit the station at platform no. 1, turn left
on Via Marsala, first right onto Via Vicenza, no. 42 is on the left
Alessandro Downtown Hostel ⓐ Via C Cattaneo 23 (Piazza Venezia &
Capitoline Hill) ☎ 06 443 40147 ⓦ www.hostelalessandrodowntown.com
ⓝ Metro: Termini Station, exit the station at platform no. 22, turn left
on Via Giolitti, second right onto Via Cattaneo, no. 23 is on the left

Beehive £ A small, cosy hostel with six double rooms, one triple and
one dormitory room that sleeps eight. ⓐ Via Marghera 8 (Piazza
Venezia & Capitoline Hill) ☎ 06 447 04553 ⓦ www.the-beehive.com
ⓝ Bus: 16, 36, 38, 40, 64, 75, 84, 86, 90, 92, 105, 170, 175, 217, 310, 360,
492, 649, 714, 910, H; Metro: Termini

Fawlty Towers £ A tongue-in-cheek name but service is considerably
better than its TV counterpart. There's a mix of dormitory and
double rooms, some with en suite facilities, as well as a communal
kitchen, internet access and a good location next door to Termini
Station. ⓐ Via Magenta 39 (Piazza Venezia & Capitoline Hill)
☎ 06 445 0374 or 06 445 4802 ⓦ www.fawltytowers.org ⓝ Bus: 16, 36,
38, 40, 64, 75, 84, 86, 90, 10, 170, 175, 217, 310, 360, 492, 649, 714, 910, H;
Metro: Termini

CAMPSITES
Understandably Rome's campsites are located outside the city, so
bear in mind travelling time when booking.

Camping Tiber £ Spacious and friendly, with swimming pool and
hot showers. Free shuttle service to and from nearby Prima Porta
Station every 30 minutes, 08.00–23.00. ⓐ Via Tiberina, KM 1,400

ⓘ 06 336 10733 ⓦ www.campingtiber.com Ⓜ Metro: from Termini Station take the A line towards the Flaminio stop, exit the train there and change to the F line on the above ground metro. Get off at the Prima Porta stop and take the shuttle bus to the campground.

Flaminio Village £ Modern facilities, swimming pool and the closest site to the city centre. ⓐ Via Flaminia Nuova 821 ⓘ 06 333 2604 Ⓜ Take Tram no. 2 to Piazza Mancini, then transfer to bus no. 200, ask the driver to drop you at the '*fermata più vicina al campeggio*'. From Termini Station, take metro line A to Flaminio. From there take the local train to Prima Porta, alighting at Due Ponti

SELF-CATERING

Rome is one of the best cities in which to rent a holiday apartment, and it offers both a good-value option as well as a more personalised feel than a hotel. All the places listed here have websites offering pictures of the accommodation. Also check out the bi-weekly magazine *Wanted in Rome* (see page 30).

City Apartments ⓘ 06 978 45999 ⓦ www.roma.cityapartments.it

Enjoy Rome ⓐ Via Marghera 8a ⓘ 06 445 1843 ⓦ www.enjoyrome.com

Landmark Trust Apartment overlooking the Spanish Steps. Sleeps four. ⓐ Piazza di Spagna ⓘ UK (01628) 825 925 ⓦ www.landmarktrust.org.uk

Rome Sweet Home ⓐ Via delle Vite 32 ⓘ 06 699 24833 ⓦ www.romesweethome.it

The Tourist Friend ⓘ 06 682 10410 ⓦ www.bandbinrome.com

THE BEST OF ROME

So many sights, so little time. The best thing to do in Rome is to enjoy the city at an easy pace; you're never going to be able to see it all in just one visit, and even if you do you'll end up history-lagged. Pick and choose what interests you the most and let the beauty of what you see sink in. Then throw a coin in the Trevi Fountain, which will ensure you return.

TOP 10 ATTRACTIONS

- **Vatican City and St Peter's Basilica** An independent and sovereign state with the principal shrine of the Catholic Church (see page 98)

- **Piazza Navona** Rome's most famous square is also its vibrantly beating heart (see page 76)

- **Spanish Steps (Scalinata di Spagna)** A stunning set of steps that has a truly intriguing history (see page 77)

◆ *St Peter's Square is the place to congregate*

Suggested itineraries

HALF-DAY: ROME IN A HURRY

Head to the Roman Forum (see page 82) to get a sense of what life was like during the Roman Republic. This was home to political and religious institutions, shops and markets, and remained the most important area until the Republic became an empire in 50 BC and Julius Caesar built the Imperial Fora (see page 94) nearby.

1 DAY: TIME TO SEE A LITTLE MORE

Continue the ancient Rome itinerary with the Palatine Hill and the Colosseum (see page 92). At the bottom of the hill turn right at the Arch of Titus to get to the main entrance of the Colosseum. Clinging to the side of the hill are the ruins of the Baths of Septimius Severus.

One of the crown jewels in Rome's ancient monuments is the Colosseum. Awe-inspiring, it needs little historical knowledge to explain its function. Imagine the clanging of the gladiators, cries of the Christians and the roar of the crowds. After each battle or sacrifice sand was thrown on the arena floor to soak up the blood. To avoid the crowds visit in the early morning or late afternoon.

2–3 DAYS: TIME TO SEE MUCH MORE

Walk behind the Pantheon (see page 75) to Piazza della Minerva and you will find Bernini's diminutive and whimsical *Elephant Statue*. The obelisk on the elephant's back is a reference to the reign of Pope Alexander VII, to illustrate the fact that strength supports wisdom. In front of you is the grand façade of **Santa Maria sopra Minerva** (❶ 06 679 3926), the only Gothic church in Rome, built in the late 13th century over the ruins of a temple to Minerva. Inside is the Carafa Chapel with its fresco of *The Assumption* by Filippino Lippi and, on the left side of the altar, Michelangelo's *Christ Bearing the Cross*, c. 1521.

The Fontana di Trevi (Trevi Fountain) and the Spanish Steps (see page 77) have been drawing tourists since the 18th century when Rome was on the itinerary of the Grand Tour. The Trevi Fountain was begun by Salvi in 1732 and finished in 1762 by Pannini. It is a massive baroque creation: Neptune stands in a shell chariot pulled by horses in front of a triumphal arch (see page 70).

A good place to find some shade on a sweltering summer day is the Villa Borghese, a series of parks that form the core of Rome's largest central open space. Made up of the grounds of the 17th-century *palazzo* of Cardinal Scipione Borghese, it's a huge area, with a boating lake, a zoo and three of the city's finest museums. The informative website is worth checking: Ⓦ www.villaborghese.it

The Piazza Navona (see page 76) is crowded day and night with tourists, street musicians, buskers and artists. Hang out at the fountains or pricey cafés with those who want to see and be seen.

LONGER: ENJOYING ROME TO THE FULL

Allow several days to explore the Vatican (see page 98); Castel Sant'Angelo, St Peter's Basilica, the gardens, galleries and museums all make up the richest but most exhausting museum complex in the world.

The Sistine Chapel (see page 104), a barn-like structure built between 1473 and 1481 for Pope Sixtus IV, is the Pope's private chapel. The ceiling and wall murals here are regarded by many as the greatest masterpieces in Western art executed by one man, Michelangelo. An average day brings in excess of 20,000 visitors to the chapel.

Something for nothing

Rome can be as expensive or inexpensive as you want it to be. In fact the cheapest and most enjoyable pastime in Rome is simply walking around the city's piazzas, parks, outdoor artwork, monuments, fountains, ancient architecture and colourful gardens.

Many churches, particularly those located in out-of-the-way neighbourhoods, are free, offering a splendid chance to see beautiful interiors and liturgical artwork.

During *Settimana dei Beni Culturali* (Cultural Heritage Week, see page 9) state-owned museums throughout Rome are open to the public at no charge.

Many museums also offer free admission on the last Sunday of the month: check with the tourist board, local listings and newspapers.

From June to September there are free performances of music, dance and opera at many of the city's open parks and squares.

Something new that's catching on well at wine shops are *degustazione* (wine tastings), which offer a chance to sample new, interesting vintages, often at no cost. At the cocktail hour, bistros and cafés put out tempting food samplings, so dust off your backpacks, change your clothes and join the foray – for the price of a drink you can dine well.

Festas (festivals) are a Roman way of life, bringing a huge number of free events to enjoy: music, parades, live theatre, fireworks and food. In mid-August everything shuts down for two weeks to celebrate *Ferragosto* (the Feast of the Assumption). The entire city is rife with celebrations, parades, hot-air balloon rides and music jam sessions, to name just a few events. Streets are clogged with food kiosks where you can eat free, or very inexpensively, on wonderful specialities such as *calamari* (squid), fresh pasta dishes, cheeses, *gelato* (ice cream) and pastries.

Or, when in Rome do as the Romans do and simply people-watch from an outdoor café or the steps of an ancient church.

⬥ *The fourth-century San Sebastiano church has a rich history*

When it rains

There's no need to let the odd shower dampen your enthusiasm for this glorious city. Your rainy-day options could well include some of the imperial city's more intriguing possibilities.

The **Catacombe di San Callisto** (Catacomb of St Callixtus, ⓐ Via Appia Antica 110–126 ⓣ 06 513 01580) is a splendidly creepy idea. Rome has many catacombs (underground burial vaults), but these are the largest; they house the remains of St Callixtus, and other early popes are buried here in the papal crypt. Some of the walls are also decorated with frescoes.

Down the road from St Callixtus, in a basilica built by Emperor Constantine, are the **Catacombe di San Sebastiano** (Catacombs of St Sebastian, ⓐ Via Appia Antica 136 ⓐ 06 785 0350). It is believed that the remains of Saints Peter and Paul were hidden here to protect them from the vile intentions of body snatchers until they could be moved on to their final resting places. A statue of St Sebastian adorns his tomb, and opposite this is a slab of marble that is allegedly imprinted with the footprints of Christ. The walls contain paintings of doves and fish, which were symbols of Christianity in early times.

In AD 64 a fire ravaged Rome destroying much of the city, and the narcissistic Emperor Nero took advantage of the event to secure for himself large swathes of land to build his own Golden House, the **Domus Aurea** (ⓐ Via della Domus Aurea ⓣ 06 397 49907 ⓘ Booking essential). It was never intended as a residence, but as a series of banquet halls, sunken baths, terraces and gardens. Everything about the house was extravagant, and, to the modern aesthetic, not a little camp. Built on 80 hectares (200 acres), facing a lake, the façade was gilded with solid gold. Inside features included indoor plumbing and even a pump that emitted perfume into the air to 'decorate' honoured guests. Nero's self-importance was also illustrated by the 45 m (150 ft) nude statue of himself at the entrance. Nero committed suicide in AD 68, and the house was eventually destroyed to make way for the Colosseum (see page 92). It wasn't until the 14th century that the remains of walls were discovered, decorated with frescoes that were later to inspire Raphael and other Renaissance painters.

⬤ *Take a tour of Nero's Domus Aurea*

On arrival

Air and train are the best ways to arrive in Rome. Arrival by bus or
car will be met with the legendary traffic congestion.

TIME DIFFERENCE

Italy is on Central European Time (CET). During Daylight Saving Time
(late Mar–late Oct), clocks are set one hour ahead.

ARRIVING

By air

Rome is serviced by two airports. Leonardo da Vinci International,
known as Fiumicino, is located 30 km (19 miles) southwest of the
city and handles most scheduled flights. Ciampino, 15 km (10 miles)
southeast of Rome, is the airport of choice for both charter and
budget airlines. **Aeroporti di Roma** (Ⓦ www.adr.it) provides live
flight information for both airports and timetables in English.

There are three terminals at Fiumicino Airport: A for domestic
flights, B for international flights within the EU, and C for all other
international flights. The airport is connected to the city by trains
to Termini Station, which take 30 minutes. They cost €11, and the
service begins at 06.36, leaving every half hour until 23.36. A slightly
cheaper option is to take a train to Ostiense or Tiburtina, then take
city bus no. 175 from Ostiense, or bus no. 492 or 649 from Tiburtina
to the city centre.

The city's second aiport, Ciampino Airport, does not have a rail
connection. If you arrive on one of the budget airlines, take their
shuttle bus that leaves 30 minutes after each arrival for Termini
Station. Another option is the COTRAL buses that run every 30 minutes
from the airport to the Anagnina metro station, at the end of metro

line A. The 30-minute trip costs approx. €1.30, and from there it's a 20-minute ride into the city, which costs approx. €1.00.

Taxis are the most convenient but most expensive way of getting to and from the airport. Agree on a fare beforehand and make sure the meter is running. Taxis into the city centre from either airport cost around €40, taking 30 minutes from Fiumicino and 45 minutes from Ciampino.

○ *Look for the Museum of Architecture by Termini Station*

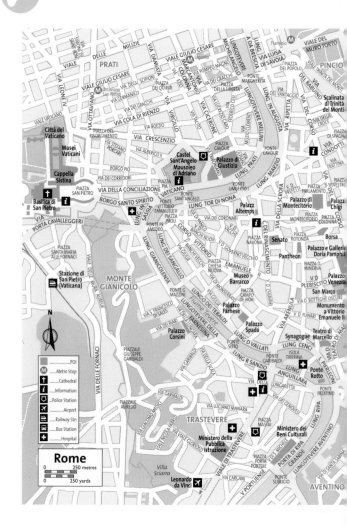

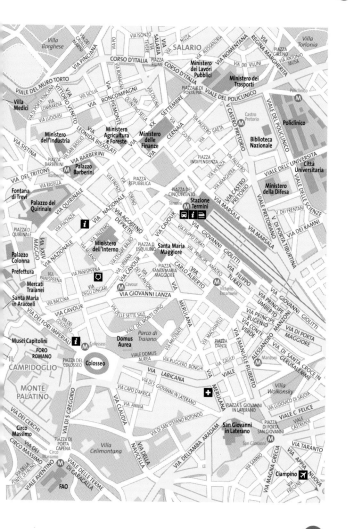

By rail
Stazione Termini (ⓐ Piazza dei Cinquecento ⓣ 06 489 06300
ⓦ www.romatermini.it) – more commonly known as Termini – is the
main railway station in Rome, and the one at which you are likely to
arrive when travelling by train to Rome. Both metro lines pass through
and many of the bus routes terminate here. The Termini has a left-
luggage department, which is open from 07.00–00.00 and costs
about €4 per item per five hours.

By road
There are numerous bus stations in Rome, but the main ones are outside
the following metro stations: Lepanto, Ponte Mammolo and Tiburtina
(for routes north) and Anagnina and EUR Fermi (for routes south).

Driving into Rome is not recommended – the traffic is dreadful
and parking in the city is a continual nightmare. However, if you
must drive, then follow these instructions: if coming from the north
on the A1 highway, take the Roma Nord exit, and if coming from the
south, take the Roma Est exit. Both routes culminate at the Grande
Raccordo Anulare (GRA) road which runs around the city and connects
all the major routes into Rome's city centre. From Ciampino, follow
Via Appia Nuova into the centre, or join the GRA at junction 23 and
follow the signs to the centre. From Fiumicino take the A12 motorway
into the city centre; this route crosses the river just north of the
suburb EUR. From there it is a short drive north up Via Cristoforo
Colombo to the city walls, and beyond to the Baths of Caracalla.

FINDING YOUR FEET
One of the best ways to orientate yourself on your first day in Rome
is to find a table at an outdoor café, absorb your surroundings, and
study your city and transit maps.

IF YOU GET LOST, TRY ...

Excuse me, do you speak English?
Mi scusi, parla inglese?
Mee skoozee, parrla eenglehzeh?

Excuse me, is this the right way to the old town/the city centre/the tourist office/the station/the bus station?
Mi scusi, questa è la strada giusta per la città vecchia/
il centro/l'ufficio informazioni turistiche/la stazione ferroviaria/
la stazione degli autobus?
*Mee skoozee, kwestah eh lah strahdah justah pehr la cheetah
vehkyah/eel chentroh/loofeecho eenfohrmahtsyonee
tooreesteekah/lah stahtsyoneh fehrohveeahreeah/
lah stahtsyoneh dehlyee owtohboos?*

Treat Rome as you would any other large city, employing normal levels of common sense. Near the train station and Piazza Repubblica (and on buses) hold your belongings firmly under your arm and wear any rucksacks around your front. Be conscious of your surroundings, and do not carry large sums of money, cameras or jewellery. After dark, take taxis or walk only in well-lit areas. Rome is full of motor scooters whose drivers are experts at snatching pedestrians' purses, cameras or necklaces. Keep all valuables out of sight.

ORIENTATION
Rome's city centre is divided into blocks. The web of streets making up the *centro storico* (historic centre) occupies a spit of land on the left bank of the River Tiber, bordered on the east by Via del Corso and

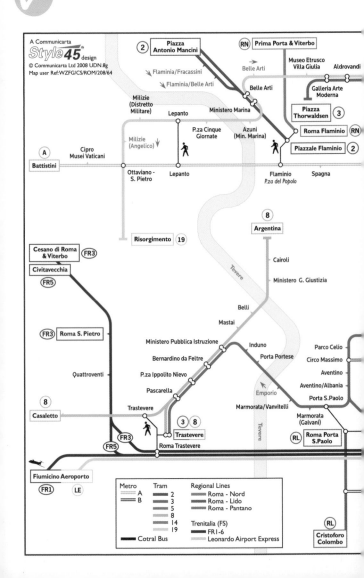

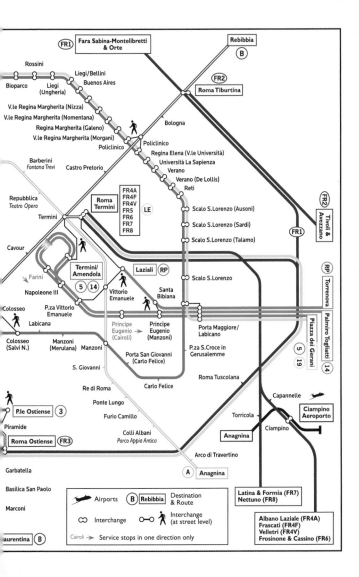

the north and south by water. Spreading east from here is Rome's central core, across the Via del Corso to the major shopping streets and alleyways that surround the Spanish Steps, down to Via Nazionale and beyond to the ancient city in the south and to Villa Borghese park to the north. The left bank of the river is home to the Vatican and St Peter's, while to the south of these is the neighbourhood of Trastevere, the heart of the city centre's nightlife. It can be quite easy to lose your way, particularly if you head down the many alleyways that entice with sounds and smells, so always carry a map.

GETTING AROUND

The best way to get around the city centre and ancient sites is by walking. Use public transport for longer trips to the Galleria Borghese, the Vatican Museums and Trastevere, the neighbourhoods of Testaccio, EUR, the catacombs, the excavations at Ostia and Tivoli, or to nearby beaches.

Agencia dei Transport Autogerro-tranviari del Commune di Roma (ATAC) run the city's bus, tram and metro system. The free enquiries line (☎ 800 431 784) is open 08.00–18.00 Mon–Fri; its website (🌐 www.atac.roma.it) has tourist information in English. Electric minibuses negotiate the narrow backstreets of the old centre. After midnight night buses access most parts of the city until 05.30. Night buses can be identified by an 'N' before the number and an owl symbol above the *bus notturno* timetable. Tickets can be purchased on board.

The bus and tram system is efficient and easy to use, and runs from 05.30–00.00 daily. It also prevents having to deal with Rome's notorious traffic. You can buy a transport map at any *edicola* (newspaper kiosk).

You can buy a flat-fare ticket for €1.00. This ticket is valid for as many bus and tram rides as you want, and one metro ride within

75 minutes of validation of the ticket. ❶ You need to punch your ticket on all buses and trams (there are yellow ticket-punching machines on each bus and tram) or you will be fined.

Tickets are available at the ATAC office, newsstands, tobacconists, and at ticket machines located in all metro stations and at major bus stops. One-, three- and seven-day passes are available for €4, €11 and €16 respectively. One-day passes allow unlimited public transport travel in the city until midnight of the day bought. ❶ There are hefty fines, around €50, for dodging fares.

If you are planning to travel outside Rome the BIRG regional transport passes for COTRAL and ATAC services, available in the metro, and at tobacconists and newsstands, are good value. Prices depend on which type of pass you buy. Discounts apply to children under ten, students, disabled people and senior citizens over 70.

Rome's metro (Ⓦ www.metroroma.it) runs from 05.30–23.30 week days and until 01.30 on Friday and Saturday, but in terms of sightseeing it's not that useful. There are only two lines – A (orange) and B (blue) – which are really designed for transporting working

🔺 *The electric minibus is a convenient way to reach the Villa Borghese*

commuters in and out of the city. A new C line is under construction, but its first section will not open until 2013. Termini is the hub for these lines, and there are stations at the Colosseum, Piazza Barberini and Piazza di Spagna.

Taxis can be radio-paged by calling ☏ 06 3570, 06 4994 or 06 6645. Be aware that you will have to pay for the driver's time to reach you as well as for the journey itself.

Only yellow or white taxis are fully licensed and equipped with a card, in English, showing the rates and extra charges for luggage, any journeys between 22.00 and 07.00, Sundays and holidays. There are fixed rates for journeys to and from the airport. Prices start at €2.33 from Monday to Saturday (€3.36 on Sunday and holidays), with an additional charge of €0.78 per km.

CAR HIRE

No tourist should even consider driving in Rome proper – parking is limited and non-residents are not even allowed to drive in the city centre in an attempt to curb the traffic. However, you can rent a car to explore the countryside. Ask your air carrier if it offers a fly/drive package. All of the following have agencies at Fiumicino airport.

AutoEurope has several offices in Rome. ☏ 800 123 704
🖅 www.autoeurope.it
Avis ⓐ Via Giovanni Giolitti 34, Stazione Termini ☏ 06 481 4373
🖅 www.avis.com Ⓜ Metro: Termini
Hertz ⓐ Via Vittorio Veneto 156 ☏ 06 488 0049 🖅 www.hertz.com
Ⓜ Metro: Barberini
Maggiore ⓐ Via Giovanni Giolitti, Stazione Termini ☏ 06 229 35356

▶ *You can't miss Rome's ancient sports arena: the Colosseum*

THE CITY OF
Rome

Piazza Venezia & Capitoline Hill

This part of Rome encompasses areas that have been especially significant to the city's history. Capitoline Hill was the political hub of the Empire, the Washington, DC of its day. The Piazza Venezia, by contrast, was of iconic importance to two of Rome's subsequent would-be empire builders.

SIGHTS & ATTRACTIONS

Il Campidoglio (Capitoline Hill)

One of Rome's seven famous hills, Il Campidoglio was the focal point of imperial politics and still exerts an influence through its gift of the words 'capital' and 'capitol'. The hill was also once home to the Temple of Juno Moneta, over which was built the first Roman mint, giving the world the word 'money'. Today a church, the Santa Maria in Aracoeli, stands on the site.

The focal point of the area today is the Piazza del Campidoglio, originally designed by Michelangelo in 1530 under the auspices of Pope Paul III.

Nowadays Capitoline Hill is linked to the rest of the city by walkways connecting to the Vittoriano in one direction and to the Roman Forum in the other.

Piazza Venezia

It might be hard to imagine today, as you stand amid tooting car horns and watch the white-gloved policemen try to direct the traffic mayhem, that in the 15th century this busy roundabout was a peaceful and grand area dominated by the Palazzo Venezia and its grounds, built by Pope Paul II (see page 64). The *palazzo* also came to

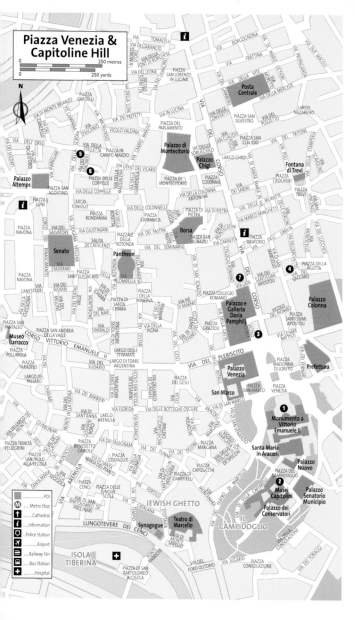

prominence in the 20th century as the place of choice for Mussolini to preach to the masses. On the opposite side of the square is the unmissable Il Vittoriano, a vast white edifice dedicated to King Vittorio Emmanuele II, and often nicknamed 'the wedding cake' and 'the typewriter'.

This busy square is an excellent place to start your exploration of Rome. It is close to the medieval and Renaissance sections of the city and the ruins of the ancient city.

CULTURE

Musei Capitolini (Capitoline Museums)

Under the umbrella title of the Capitoline Museums, these two collections are among the most important in a city that is already awash with treasures. Housed in two Michelangelo-designed *palazzi*, the Palazzo Nuovo and Palazzo dei Conservatori, the collection began life in 1471, making it the oldest public exhibition in the world. These days it is an unmissable array of ancient works and Renaissance gems. Most of the statues and paintings are labelled in English and Italian.
🅐 Piazza del Campidoglio 1 🕿 06 820 59127 🅦 www.museicapitolini.org
🕘 09.00–20.00 Tues–Sun 🅝 Bus: 30, 40, 44, 46, 62, 63, 64, 70, 81, 85, 87, 95, 117, 170, 175, 492, 628, 780, 810, 850. Admission charge
🅘 No credit cards

Palazzo dei Conservatori

On the western side of the square, the Palazzo dei Conservatori, formerly the medieval magistrates' court, is the bigger of the two museums, with its focus on statuary and 16th- and 17th-century artworks. Highlights of the first floor include frescoes such as Pietro da Cortona's *Rape of the Sabines*, one of the original bronze statues of the *Lo Spinario* collection and a marble bust of Medusa.

The second floor is dominated by Renaissance paintings from the 14th century to the 17th century, of which the best known are Caravaggio's shockingly sensual *St John the Baptist* (c. 1596), Tintoretto's *Penitent Magdalene* (c. 1598), *Baptism of Christ* (c. 1512) by Titian and *Head of a Boy* by Bolognese artist Ludovico Carraci.

Also on the second floor is an enormous picture by Guercino, *The Burial of Santa Petronilla* (1621–3), depicting an early Roman martyr who purportedly was the daughter of St Peter, originally commissioned to hang in St Peter's Basilica.

The oversized third-century fragments of a statue of Emperor Constantine are the main feature of the ground floor.

⬤ *The Capitoline Museums can't fail to impress*

PALAZZO NUOVO

Dominating the eastern flank of the Piazza del Campidoglio, the Palazzo Nuovo is accessible from the Palazzo dei Conservatori via a tunnel filled with more sculpture and the remains of a Roman temple.

And sculpture really is the order of the day in this smaller of the two museums. Highlights of the ground floor include *Marforio*, a stone depiction of the river god overlooking the courtyard fountain, plus two versions of a bronze statue of Marcus Aurelius – the second-century original and a copy.

Don't miss the Gabinetto della Venere on the first floor, dedicated entirely to the first-century BC *Capitolini Venus*, a delicate piece based on Praxiteles' *Venus of Knidos*. Another Praxiteles copy is the marble second-century BC *Resting Satyr*, which is purported to have inspired the Nathaniel Hawthorne novel *The Marble Faun*. Other highlights include the *Mosaic of the Doves* (which once adorned Hadrian's Villa), the Hall of the Philosophers (among which is the marble bust of Homer), and the poignant *Dying Gaul*, based on a third-century BC Greek original.

Palazzo Venezia

On the western side of Piazza Venezia, but with its main entrance on Via del Plebiscito, is the eponymous 15th-century Palazzo Venezia, one of the first Renaissance buildings to be constructed in Rome. If it looks strangely familiar it's probably because you've seen wartime images of Mussolini grinding home his political theories to the masses from the balcony here – the Fascist dictator took over the *palazzo* as his party headquarters. These days its focus is more on culture than chaos as home to an important collection of Renaissance arts and crafts. Not all works are open to public view, but those paintings that can be seen are some of Italy's most important 15th-century works, such as a portrait of two young men by Giorgione, Borgianni's 16th-century *Deposition of Christ* and Algardi's bust of Pope Innocent X.

● *The Roman emperor Marcus Aurelius sits on Capitoline Hill*

🔴 Via del Plebiscito 118 🕐 08.30–19.00 Tues–Sun 🔵 Bus: 30, 40, 44, 46, 62, 63, 64, 70, 81, 85, 87, 95, 117, 170, 175, 492, 628, 780, 810, 850. Admission charge

⬤ The Vittorio Emanuele Monument is one of Rome's best-loved sights

San Marco

Next to Palazzo Venezia, on the southern side of the square, is the church of San Marco, a small basilica, built in AD 336 reportedly on the site of the house where St Mark the Evangelist stayed. The façade is recognisable by the statues of lions, the symbol of St Mark, flanking the main entrance. These are almost the only relics of the original medieval church, as well as the 11th-century bell tower and an impressive mosaic depicting the life of Christ dating from the ninth century.

The church was rebuilt in the fifth century and was again reorganised by Pope Paul II in the 15th century when he built Palazzo Venezia. During this time he added his own coat of arms to decorate the church ceiling. It was given its baroque look in the mid-18th century.

In the portico is the gravestone of Vanozza Catanei, mistress of Rodrigo Borgia, Pope Alexander VI, and mother of the infamous Cesare and Lucretia Borgia. ➌ Piazza San Marco ❶ 06 679 5205 ❷ 08.30–12.30, 16.00–19.00, closed Mon am & Wed pm ⓝ Bus: 30, 40, 44, 46, 62, 63, 64, 70, 81, 85, 87, 95, 117, 170, 175, 492, 628, 780, 810, 850

Monumento a Vittorio Emanuele II (Vittorio Emanuele Monument)

One of the most famous images of Rome is *L'Altare della Patria* (Vittorio Emanuele Monument). The Vittoriano, as it is known, is built of dazzling white marble excavated from Brescia, and is a flamboyant monument to the first king of Italy after the Unification of 1870. Begun in 1885, its finishing touches were added in 1911.

On either side of the entrance are figures that represent the two seas that surround the Italian peninsula – the Tyrrhenian on the right and the Adriatic on the left. At the top of the stairs is Italy's Tomb of the Unknown Soldier fanned by an eternal flame. Crowning this is a colossal and majestic statue of King Vittorio Emanuele II on horseback; the king's moustache alone measures 3 m (10 ft) in length.

The platform it stands on has a frieze depicting figures representing the capital cities of the Italian Republic, while above it the vast pillared gallery stretches the width of the monument with figures symbolising the regions of Italy.

Inside, the exhibits are also dedicated to the Unification of Italy. The Museo del Risorgimento (Museum of the Resurgence) documents all manner of details of the more than 20-year struggle to unify the country, including a boot worn by patriot leader Giuseppe Garibaldi when he was shot in the foot in 1862. There are excellent explanations in both English and Italian that help visitors to understand all the key events and people that took part in the *Risorgimento* ('resurgence'). **ⓐ** Piazza Venezia **ⓣ** 06 699 1718 **ⓦ** www.museodelrisorgimento.mi.it **ⓛ** Monument 09.30–16.00, Museo del Risorgimento 09.30–18.30 **ⓝ** Bus: 30, 40, 44, 46, 62, 63, 64, 70, 81, 85, 87, 95, 117, 170, 175, 492, 628, 780, 810, 850. Admission charge **ⓘ** No credit cards

RETAIL THERAPY

This area of the city might appear to be a traffic bottleneck – which it is – but nevertheless shopping here is surprisingly fruitful. You will find everything from designer gear to replicas of ancient statuary.

Diesel Trendy styles geared towards 20- and 30-somethings. **ⓐ** Via del Corso 186 **ⓣ** 06 678 3933 **ⓛ** 09.30–19.30 Mon–Sat **ⓝ** Bus: 30, 40, 44, 46, 62, 63, 64, 70, 81, 85, 87, 95, 117, 170, 175, 492, 628, 780, 810, 850

Energie One of Rome's most popular stores, aimed primarily at teenagers and 20-somethings with expensive and trendy tastes in fashion. **ⓐ** Via del Corso 486 **ⓣ** 06 322 7046 **ⓛ** 10.00–20.00

🕙 Bus: 30, 40, 44, 46, 62, 63, 64, 70, 81, 85, 87, 95, 117, 170, 175, 492, 628, 780, 810, 850

MAS Several floors here are crammed to the rafters offering everything from clothing to household items. 🅐 Piazza Vittorio Emanuele 138 ☎ 06 446 6078 🕙 09.00–13.00, 15.45–19.45 Mon–Sat 🕙 Bus: 30, 40, 44, 46, 62, 63, 64, 70, 81, 85, 87, 95, 117, 170, 175, 492, 628, 780, 810, 850

TAKING A BREAK

Museums and shopping are all very well but they do have a habit of whipping up a thirst and an appetite, so take time out to relax every so often at the various appealing cafés in the area.

Café Aracoeli £ ❶ This pleasant outdoor café is halfway up the terraces of the Vittoriano and affords good views along with refreshment. 🅐 Piazza Venezia ☎ 06 699 1718 🕙 09.30–19.30 Mon–Sat 🕙 Bus: 30, 40, 44, 46, 62, 63, 64, 70, 81, 85, 87, 95, 117, 170, 175, 492, 628, 780, 810, 850

Café at Musei Capitolini £ ❷ Museum cafés don't often engender much gastronomic enthusiasm, but this one bucks the trend. There are also knockout views from the outdoor terrace. 🅐 Piazza del Campidoglio 1 ☎ 06 820 59127 🕙 09.00–20.00 Tues–Sun; closed 1 January, 1 May, 25 December 🕙 Bus: 30, 40, 44, 46, 62, 63, 64, 70, 81, 85, 87, 95, 117, 170, 175, 492, 628, 780, 810, 850

Caffè Napoleon Venezia £ ❸ Good for a mid-morning break, as well as a light lunch. 🅐 Via del Corso 🕙 08.00–midnight

Ⓝ Bus: 30, 40, 44, 46, 62, 63, 64, 70, 81, 85, 87, 95, 117, 170, 175, 492, 628, 780, 810, 850

AFTER DARK

Abruzzi £ ❹ Veal is the speciality at this good-value restaurant whose prices attract students, so expect a lively atmosphere. ⓐ Via del Vaccaro 1 ⓣ 06 679 3897 ⓛ 12.30–15.00, 19.00–23.00 Sun–Fri Ⓝ Bus: 44, 46 ❶ Closed three weeks in August

Alfredo alla Scrofa ££ ❺ One of the two places in Rome that claims to have created *fettucine Alfredo* (pasta in a cream and garlic sauce); also serves excellent meat dishes. ⓐ Via della Scrofa ⓣ 06 688 06163 ⓛ 12.30–15.00, 19.00–23.30 Ⓝ Bus: 87, 492, 680; Metro: Piazza di Spagna

Caffè Riccioli ££ ❻ This Japanese restaurant boasts stylish dining rooms and platters of excellent *sashimi*, along with beef and seafood dishes and delicious desserts. ⓐ Piazza delle Coppelle 10a ⓣ 06 682 10313 ⓛ 12.00–02.00 Ⓝ Bus: 64, 92; Tram: 8; Metro: Piazza di Spagna

Trinity College Irish Pub ££ ❼ Every city in the world now boasts an Irish pub, and this noisy establishment offers a variety of beers, including Guinness. ⓐ Via del Collegio Romano 6 ⓣ 06 678 6472 ⓛ 12.00–03.00 Ⓝ Bus: 30, 40, 46, 62, 64, 70, 81, 87, 116, 492, 628

◐ *The Trevi Fountain in Piazza di Trevi: the most famous fountain in Rome*

Centro Storico (Historic Centre)

In a city that is so intrinsically linked to history at almost every corner, it seems absurd to pinpoint one area as the 'historic centre'. Nevertheless, Centro Storico is the name that is applied to the triangular region around Piazza Navona and surrounded by Rome's main streets (Corso Vittorio Emanuele II and Via del Corso) and the River Tiber. It's a wonderful area in which to spend a day strolling its many alleyways and admiring some of the city's best examples of classical and baroque architecture. The following sights and attractions are presented in the order we suggest you visit them for maximum enjoyment.

SIGHTS & ATTRACTIONS

Piazza Campo de' Fiori

In the rough and tumble world of the Middle Ages, right through to the Renaissance, the Campo de' Fiori (literally 'field of flowers') was a hive of activity due to its daily market. But it was also a place of intrigue, murder and execution. Among those who met their fate here was the 16th-century philosopher Giordano Bruno, who stood firm against the Inquisition and was burned at the stake in return. Today a statue of the martyr is the focal point of the square.

Following long-standing tradition, there is still a bustling market here every morning, offering a wonderful array of colours from the numerous fruit and vegetable stalls. It's a fascinating place to enjoy an outdoor drink at one of the many cafés on the square and soak up the atmosphere. ⓐ Piazza Campo de'Fiori ⓛ 07.00–13.00 Mon–Sat ⓝ Bus: 30, 40, 62, 64, 70, 81, 87, 116, 492, 571, 628

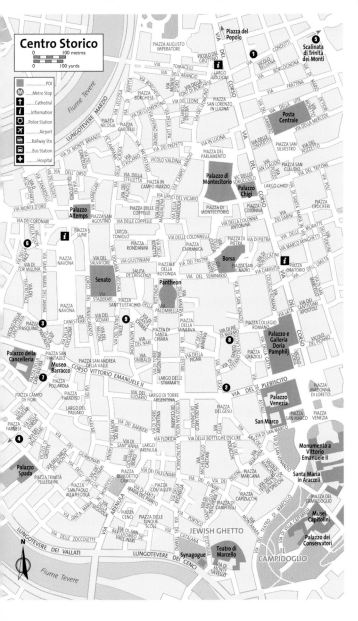

Jewish Ghetto

Situated to the east of Via Arenula is the area historically known as the Jewish Ghetto. Rome's Jewish population dates back to the second century BC, and for centuries they were integrated into society with little or no prejudice. All this was to change, however, during the period of the Inquisition and the Counter-Reformation, and between 1555 and 1559 Pope Paul VI ordered that the entire Jewish community must live within a walled and decidedly unpleasant enclosure. From then on, right up until the Unification of Italy, and as a chilling precursor to what would happen some 500 years later, any Jew venturing out of the ghetto was required to wear a yellow cap and shawl as a means of religious identification.

Today the former ghetto is home to Rome's largest **synagogue**, (🕐 10.00–17.00 Sun–Thur (until 19.00 June–Sept); closed Jewish hols) which contains a fascinating insight into the history of the building and the Jewish community of the city. Entry is by guided tour (in English) only – the synagogue was attacked by the Palastine Liberation Organisation (PLO) in 1982, and has been under police guard ever since.

Palazzo Altemps

Another important Roman family, the Altemps, bought this 15th-century *palazzo* in 1568 and, again, used it to house and expand their impressive art collection. In 1997, following a painstaking restoration, the building was incorporated into the Museo Nazionale Romano as a home for a breathtaking collection of classical sculpture.

Much of the collection was acquired in the 17th century by Cardinal Ludovico Ludovisi. Among the masterpieces are a bust of the philosopher Demosthenes from the second century AD, a statue entitled *Athena with Serpent* and a Roman copy of a Greek *Galata's*

Suicide, which is thought to have been commissioned by Julius Caesar. There is also a statue of Ares that was repaired by Bernini in 1621, and several erotic works, the delightful *Pan and Daphne,* a Satyr and Nymph, and the muses Calliope and Urania. Additionally, there's a fifth-century BC 'throne' with carved reliefs. ⓐ Via di Sant'Apollinare 46 ⓘ 06 689 7091 ⓛ 09.00–19.45 Tues–Sun ⓐ Bus: 30, 70, 81, 87, 116, 130, 186, 492, 628. Admission charge

Pantheon

Looming down over Piazza della Rotunda, the Pantheon, along with the Colosseum, stands today as the most complete ancient Roman structure in the city. There has been a temple here since 27 BC during Marcus Agrippa's rule, but it was entirely rebuilt by the emperor Hadrian in the early second century AD.

△ The Pantheon – an almost complete ancient Roman structure

One of Hadrian's most remarkable additions was the domed roof at a staggering size of 43 m by 43 m (142 ft by 142 ft). At one time the entire roof was also cast in bronze, but this was melted down in the 17th century under the orders of Pope Urban VIII in order to make the *baldacchino* (canopy) for St Peter's Basilica in the Vatican. The Pantheon was consecrated as a church in the seventh century after the discovery of Christian bones on the site.

Since the 19th century the Pantheon has also been used as the burial place of Italian monarchs, including the first king of Italy, Vittorio Emanuele II. The artist Raphael is also buried here. ⓐ Piazza della Rotonda ⓣ 06 683 00230 ⓒ 08.30–19.30 Mon–Sat, 09.00–18.00 Sun ⓝ Bus: 40, 46, 62, 70, 87, 116, 492, 628, 810

Piazza Navona

If anywhere can be described as the heart of this rambling city, it must surely be Piazza Navona, and no visit is complete without soaking up the atmosphere of this beautiful square. The area was originally used for chariot races but the majority of its current appearance dates from the 17th century when beautiful *palazzi* and churches were commissioned by Pope Innocent X. Among the first was the church of Sant'Agnese in Agone, designed by Borromini and supposedly built on the site where the 13-year-old St Agnes was stripped naked in front of the entire city in the third century AD for her religious views.

The full length of the square is punctuated by three baroque fountains, all designed by Bernini around 1651. The central Fontana dei Quattro Fiumi (Fountain of the Four Rivers) is the most famous, with each figure representing the most important rivers in that period: the Nile, the Danube, the Ganges and the Plate. The Fontana del Moro (Fountain of the Moor) at the southern end of the square depicts, as its name suggests, the figure of a North African Moor,

SCALINATA DI TRINITA DEI MONTI (SPANISH STEPS)

These beautiful broad, tiered steps and the adjoining Piazza di Spagna get their name from the Spanish Embassy that used to have its headquarters here. The steps were constructed in 1725 by Francisco de Sanctis as a means of reaching the Trinità dei Monti church at the top of the hill, and the three tiers were intended to reflect the three figures of the Holy Trinity.

Their popularity as a general meeting place and social spot began in the 18th century at the height of the Grand Tour period because this was the area where most of the hotels and boarding houses were located. Facing onto the Piazza di Spagna on the eastern side of the foot of the Spanish Steps is the Keats-Shelley Memorial House, set up as a library in honour of the poet John Keats, who died here at the age of 25 in 1821, and Percy Bysshe Shelley, poet and husband of *Frankenstein* author Mary Shelley. Manuscripts and mementoes of these and other Romantic poets are on display within the elegant rooms. ⓐ Trinità dei Monti
Ⓜ Metro: Spagna

Keats-Shelley Memorial House ⓐ Piazza di Spagna 26
ⓣ 06 678 4235 Ⓦ www.keats-shelley-house.org Ⓛ 09.00–13.00, 15.00–18.00 Mon–Fri, 11.00–14.00, 15.00–18.00 Sat; guided tours by appointment Ⓜ Metro: Spagna

while the Fontana del Nettuno (Neptune's Fountain) shows the sea god wrestling with a sea monster.

Bustling day and night, the pedestrianised square is one of the most popular places in Rome to enjoy a coffee, an aperitif or a full meal, as well as an animated gossip, at one of the numerous cafés whose tables spill out onto the pavement in summer. ⊗ Bus: 70, 81, 87

From Via del Corso to the Pantheon

Via del Corso borders the historic centre on its eastern side, stretching from Piazza Venezia in the south to Piazza del Popolo to the north. A walk along this major artery offers various turn-offs to admire lovely *palazzi*, churches, squares and, above all, the Pantheon (see page 75). Shopaholics should not miss the opportunity to explore the many stylish clothing stores along Via del Corso itself and in the various off-shoot streets to the east. The street is also renowned for its antiques shops.

Over the years Via del Corso has been home to numerous notable ex-pats: the German poet Goethe once lived at no. 18, while the Romantic poet Percy Bysshe Shelley and his wife Mary resided in no. 375 (now a bank).

Just off Via del Corso, about halfway along, is Piazza Colonna, named after the impressive first-century AD column commemorating the military successes of Marcus Aurelius with a variety of carved reliefs. The square also contains the official residence of the prime minister.

CULTURE

Museo Barracco

If you're into ancient sculpture, don't miss the small but impressive collection at the Museo Barracco. There is a range of pieces from ancient Greece and Egypt including sphinxes, friezes and ceramics. ⓐ Corso Vittorio Emanuele II 166 ❶ 06 688 06848 ⓛ 09.00–19.00 Tues–Sun ⊗ Bus: 40, 46, 62, 64, 116, 492, 571, 916. Admission charge

Palazzo & Galleria Doria Pamphilj

One of Rome's most important families, the Doria Pamphiljs, has been in ownership of this 15th-century *palazzo* since 1647. Today the family's spectacular art collection is open to public view, and includes works by Masters from all over Europe. Highlights include portraits of Pope Innocent X by Bernini and Velázquez, Dutch and Flemish artworks including Hans Memling's *Deposition*, two paintings by Caravaggio (*Mary Magdalene* and *John the Baptist*), and Titian's *Salome With the Head of St John*. Furnishings include Venetian chandeliers and Belgian tapestries. ⓐ Piazza del Collegio Romano 2 ❶ 06 679 7323 ⓦ www.doriapamphilj.it ❶ 10.00–17.00 Fri–Wed Ⓝ Bus: 62, 63, 81, 85, 117, 119, 160, 175, 492, 628, 850. Admission charge

RETAIL THERAPY

Via Condotti, just south of Piazza di Spagna, is one of the best known shopping streets in Rome and is definitely the place to come if you're after the big names in Italian fashion, jewellery and leather goods.

Borse Scultura In the student district of San Lorenzo (to the east of the train station) Claudio Sanò makes exquisitely handcrafted leather bags. A women's bag with a fulsome set of red lips stands out, but there are more classical pieces. ⓐ Largo degli Osci 67a ❶ 06 446 9284 ❶ 16.00–19.30 Mon, 10.00–13.00, 16.00–19.30 Tues–Sat Ⓝ Bus: 71, 140, 492; Tram: 3, 19

Bulgari If you're not among the lucky few who can afford these jewellery prices, the window designs are worth seeing. ⓐ Via Condotti 10 ❶ 06 69 62 61 ❶ 15.30–19.30 Mon, 10.30–19.30 Tues–Sat Ⓝ Metro: Spagna

Campanile One of the best places for high-quality, if expensive, leather goods such as handbags and belts. ⓐ Via Condotti 58 ⓣ 06 678 3041 ⓛ 15.30–19.30 Mon, 10.30–19.30 Tues–Sat ⓝ Metro: Spagna

Diego Percossi Papi For a stunning necklace, bracelet or any other jewellery visit this shop specialising in Renaissance designs. ⓐ Piazza Sant' Eustachio 16 ⓣ 06 688 01466 ⓦ www.percossipapi.com ⓛ 16.00–19.30 Mon, 10.00–13.00, 16.00–19.30 Tues–Sat ⓝ Bus: 40, 46, 62, 70, 87, 116, 492, 628, 810

TAKING A BREAK

Antico Caffè Greco £ ❶ Follow in the footsteps of Keats, Shelley and Wagner among others, and enjoy a cake and coffee amid baroque mirrors and plush red velvet seating. It's a bit of a tourist trap these days and there's certainly better fare elsewhere, but it is one of the best known cafés in the city, so it's worth the experience. ⓐ Via Condotti 86 ⓣ 06 679 1700 ⓛ 10.30–19.00 Sun & Mon, 09.00–19.30 Tues–Sat ⓝ Metro: Spagna

Enoteca Corsi £ ❷ An informal wine tavern that also serves filling Italian food such as pasta. ⓐ Via del Gesù 87–88 ⓣ 06 679 0821 ⓛ 12.00–15.30 Mon–Sat; closed Aug ⓝ Metro: Spagna

Cul de Sac £–££ ❸ The oldest wine bar in town with an enviable collection of wines (many to be consumed by the glass) and an interesting menu of one-off dishes, salads and mouth-watering plates of cold meats and cheeses from all over Italy. ⓐ Piazza Pasquino 73 ⓣ 06 688 01094 ⓛ 24 hrs ⓝ Bus: 30, 70, 81, 87, 116, 186, 492, 628

AFTER DARK

Thien Kim £ ❹ This Vietnamese rarity is good value for money.
ⓐ Via Giulia 201 ☎ 06 683 07832 🕐 19.30–23.00 Mon–Sat 🚌 Bus: 23,
30, 40, 46, 62, 64, 70, 81, 87, 116, 186, 204, 280, 492, 628, 916

Aurora 10 da Pino il Sommelier ££ ❺ Known for its 250 varieties
of wine from all over Italy and for its excellent fish and seafood.
ⓐ Via Aurora 10 near Via Veneto and Piazza Barberini ☎ 06 474 2779
🕐 12.00–15.00, 19.00–23.00 Tues–Sun 🚇 Metro: Barberini

Bramante ££ ❻ Housed in a beautiful 18th-century building behind
Piazza Navona, this venue offers home-made pasta and grilled meats.
ⓐ Via della Pace 25 ☎ 06 688 03916 🕐 17.30–02.00 Mon–Sat,
12.00–02.00 Sun 🚌 Bus: 44, 46, 55, 60, 61, 62, 64, 65

Ditirambo ££ ❼ A buzzy restaurant where the pasta, bread and sweets
are all made in-house. The menu is varied and will satisfy all palates.
ⓐ Piazza della Cancelleria 74 ☎ 06 687 1626 🌐 www.ristoranteditirambo.it
🕐 13.00–15.00, 19.30–23.30 (except Mon lunch) 🚌 Bus: 40, 62, 64, 116, 916

Green T ££–£££ ❽ A relaxed but upmarket Chinese restaurant that
has really raised the bar for the country's cuisine. ⓐ Via di Piè di
Marmo 28 ☎ 06 679 8628 🌐 www.green-tea.it 🕐 2.30–15.00, 19.30–
00.00 Mon–Sat 🚌 Bus: 81, 116, 117, 119, 590, 628

L'Eau Vive £££ ❾ The French cuisine here is excellent and served by
a lay sisterhood of missionary Christians who sing the *Ave Maria of
Lourdes* every night at 22.00. ⓐ Via Monterone 85, near Piazza Navona
and the Pantheon ☎ 06 688 01095 🌐 www.restaurant-eauvive.it
🕐 12.30–14.30, 19.30–22.00 Mon–Sat 🚌 Bus: 40, 64, 70, 81, 87, 116

Ancient Rome

For many visitors to Rome the most fascinating and exciting aspect is the chance to see the remains of one of the greatest civilisations ever known. Although nothing remains intact, there are a staggering number of ruins that still allow the imagination to recreate a sense of life in times gone by.

Mussolini's contributions to Rome and Italy in general are not usually considered successful, but the creation of the Via dei Fori Imperiali is the exception to the rule. It allowed the most concentrated area of ruins around the Forum to become a virtually pedestrianised 'park', leading from one historic gem to another. The following sights and attractions are presented in the order that affords the visitor maximum enjoyment.

SIGHTS & ATTRACTIONS

Foro Romano (The Roman Forum)

Just to the west of the Via dei Fori Imperiali lies arguably the city's most significant ancient sight, the Roman Forum. This was the heart and soul of the Roman Republic – a place of trade, worship, social gatherings, and political demonstrations and announcements. Even when the increasing population and importance of the city at the advent of the Imperial age required further *fora*, the Roman Forum remained of great importance to the daily life of the citizens.

One of Rome's consuls and rulers, Julius Caesar, realised the need for expansion, and constructed a new senate as well as temples and shops around 50 BC. The work that was continued after Caesar's death by his nephew and successor Augustus, and later by the Flavian emperors Vespasian, Nerva and Trajan. Gradually, however,

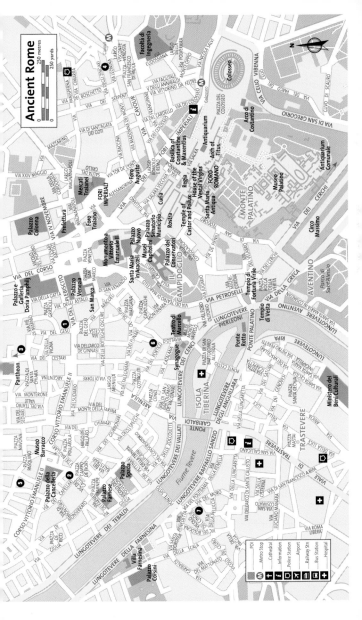

the Forum, much like the empire, began to fall into decay. Many of the buildings were destroyed by a fire in the third century AD, and within a few decades invaders such as the Visigoths left the city in disarray. Building for the future rather than preserving the past was top of the agenda for centuries, and the Forum was often stripped bare to acquire construction materials for other areas. It wasn't until the 19th century, when the burgeoning interest in archaeology was at its zenith, that the historical significance of the area was appreciated and excavations begun.

At first glance the area today may seem little more than rubble and stumps of stone, but as you gradually immerse yourself in the atmosphere it's hard not to marvel that these two hectares (five acres) were once the heart of the Mediterranean world, and the goings-on that occurred here are still of daily significance in the Western world in terms of language, architecture, law and politics. ⓐ Via dei Fori Imperiali ❶ 06 399 67700 ❷ 09.00–19.00 Apr–Sept; 09.00–16.30 Oct–Mar; last admission one hour before closing Ⓝ Bus: 60. 75, 85, 87, 117, 175, 186, 271, 571, 810; Metro: Colosseo. Admission charge

The Antiquarium & Arch of Titus On the Via Sacra, past the church of Santa Maria Nova, is the Antiquarium, the main museum of the site. Exploration of this museum will really contextualise the archaeological wonders discovered here and illustrate why the Roman Forum proved to be of such historical significance. Within the collection are statue fragments, capitals, tiles, mosaics and friezes, as well as skeletons and wooden coffins exhumed from an Iron-Age necropolis found near the Temple of Antoninus and Faustina. ❷ 09.00–one hour before sunset Tues–Sat, 09.00–16.00 Mon

◆ *The Forum was the bustling heart of the Roman Republic*

At the top of Via Sacra, thought to be the oldest road in the city, stands the impressive Arch of Titus, built by the emperor's brother Domitian after Titus's death in AD 81. It commemorates his victories in Judaea in AD 70. The structure has been restored many times, and the reliefs can still be seen depicting Titus riding in a chariot with Nike, Goddess of Victory, being escorted by the senate and the people. The opposite side shows spoils such as a Jewish menorah being removed from the Temple of Jerusalem.

The Basilica of Constantine & Maxentius Opposite the House of the Vestal Virgins (see page 88) is the Temple of Romulus, son of the Emperor Maxentius, built in AD 309. The temple serves as vestibule for the church of Santi Cosima e Damiano. Of importance here is the wonderful sixth-century apse mosaic showing Christ and the Apostles. Past the temple a walkway leads up to the Basilica of Constantine & Maxentius, named after the two emperors who oversaw its construction in the fourth century AD. Once the largest building in the Forum, it is still impressive for its size and construction. Originally it was a place for holding legal proceedings as well as a stock exchange.

The Curia (Senate House) The imposing pillared building at the western end of the Forum is the Curia, originally built by Julius Caesar but rebuilt in the third century AD under Emperor Diocletian. Its original purpose was as the Republic's Senate House and the scene of important political deliberations. At the fall of the Empire it became a church and remained in that guise until its restoration in the 20th century.

For a clearer understanding of how Roman politics had such an influence on political procedures today, venture inside and examine

Roman senators met at the Curia, the Senate House

the three wide stairs ascending left and right where some 300 Roman senators would sit on their folding chairs to discuss matters of the day. In the middle of these two staircases there's a speakers' platform with a porphyry statue of a figure wearing a toga. Most spectacular, however, not least for the fact that it has managed to survive the centuries, is the original polychrome floor in bright red, yellow, green and white marble. There are also some surviving marble reliefs depicting Emperor Trajan, most likely commissioned by the emperor himself, given the generous light in which he is portrayed. The *Plutei of Trajan* shows him getting ready to burn public record books in order to relieve Roman citizens of debts to the state; the relief to the right is equally philanthropic, showing him giving money to a woman to indicate his concern for widows and orphans.

The Lapis Niger is a stone which marks the traditional site of the tomb of Romulus. Its steps lead to a monument that was sacred ground during ancient times. The Column of Phocas, across the travertine pavement from the Curia, also known as the Rostra, was the scene of public speeches. To the right of it, the Arch of Septimius Severus was constructed in the third century by his sons Caracalla and Galba to mark their father's victories in the Middle East.

House of the Vestal Virgins Beyond the Temple of Vesta is the House of the Vestal Virgins, a second-century AD reconstruction of a building originally built by Nero. Vesta was the Roman goddess of the hearth and home who achieved a cult following during Roman times. The Vestal Virgins were six women who were selected to oversee the Temple of Vesta and keep her sacred flame alight at all times, but were ordered to remain virginal for their full time of 'office' – 30 years from the age of around ten to 40. The importance of their chastity cannot be over-emphasised – the women were buried alive and the violator murdered if they were known to have reneged on this promise. On retirement, the women were accommodated in palaces and were financially secure until their deaths.

The Regia When Italy was ruled by the Etruscans, their method of government was monarchical rather than imperial. The three steps flanking the Via Sacra belonged to the Regia, or house of kings – an ancient grouping of foundations that date from the reign of the second king of Rome, Numa, who ruled from 715 to 673 BC. There was a shrine of Mars here that housed the supposed shield and spears of the God of War, which generals embarking on a campaign would rattle before setting off. If the shields and swords rattled of their own accord, however, it was considered a bad omen, and one that required purification and repentance rites.

Across the road from here is the Temple of Antoninus and Faustina, a second-century AD temple still in a remarkable state of preservation, largely because it has been part of the church of San Lorenzo in Miranda since the seventh century. An inscribed lintel connects the six Corinthian columns across the front, dedicating the temple by order of the Senate to the god Antonino and the goddess Faustina, the parents of that great military leader Marcus Aurelius. Above the inscription is the roof architrave, along the sides of which can be seen the original frieze of griffins, candelabras and acanthus scrolls. The façade of the church dates back to 1602.

The pile of rubble that is next to the Regia is sadly all that remains of the magnificence that was thought to be the temple to Julius Caesar. A round stone stump under the roof marks the spot where Caesar was cremated after his murder and around which the temple was built.

The broken columns to the right of the Via Sacra mark the site of the Basilica Aemilia, built in the 2nd century BC as a meeting and trade centre. Nearby is a small marble plaque dedicated to Venus Cloacin, marking the site of a small shrine dedicated to Venus where the Cloaca Maxima canal drained the Forum, which was situated on marsh land. The Cloaca Maxima reaches all the way to the Tiber from here and still keeps the area drained.

The Rostra To the left of the arch is a low wall, the Rostra, one of the most important places in the entire Forum in ancient times. Citizens, traders, senators and interested bystanders gathered to hear important speeches delivered from this spot – it was here that Mark Antony gave his famous celebratory speech about Caesar following his assassination.

On the left of the Rostra are the stairs of the Basilica Julia, built by Julius Caesar as a law court in 54 BC after his triumphant return from the Gallic Wars. You cannot mount the stairs, as all that remains of the basilica are a few column bases and one nearly complete column.

Further along is the oldest temple in the Forum, the Temple of Saturn, dating from 497 BC. What remains of it are the results of a series of restorations undertaken between 42 BC and as late as AD 380. The temple housed the Roman treasury and mint, but its main focus was during the Saturnalia celebrations each December – a precursor to modern-day Christmas. To the right of this are the remaining columns of the Temple of Vespasian and Titus, built in AD 80. Behind the Arch of Septimius Severus, a pile of bricks is all that is left of the Temple of Concordia Augusta, dedicated by Tiberius in AD 10.

▶ *The Septimius Severus Arch commemorates this emperor's victories*

Santa Maria Antiqua & the Temple of Castor and Pollux Santa Maria Antiqua on Vicus Tuscus ('Etruscan Street') was the first public building in the area to be converted for Christian worship. After being closed for many years, it has recently reopened. Around the corner on the right, the flattened area topped by three Corinthian columns is the Temple of Castor and Pollux.

Colosseo (The Colosseum)

The Colosseum was built during the heyday of the Roman Empire between 70 and 80 AD. It was the largest amphitheatre in Rome, set in the centre of the city, and it originally hosted gladiatorial shows, animal hunts and other entertainment. A symbol of great Roman architecture, the construction, though partially in ruins, is still an awesome landmark. ● 09.00–one hour before sunset ● 06 399 67700 ● www.the-colosseum.net ● Bus: 60, 75, 85, 87, 117, 175, 186, 271, 571, 810; Metro: Colosseo. Admission charge

---

● *The Colosseum was the largest amphitheatre in the Roman Empire*

Fori Imperiali (Imperial Fora)

Rome is possibly the largest ongoing excavation site in the world, and digs are still underway and uncovering remarkable finds. Since the 1990s a lot of this work has concentrated on the Imperial Fora area around what is now the Via dei Fori Imperiali. The Forum of Trajan (which houses the new Imperial Fora Museum, see opposite) and the Forum of Augustus on the north side are the most interesting. The Forums of Vespasian, Nerva and Caesar are also worth a stop. A visitor centre opposite the church of Santi Cosma e Damiano offers guided tours and brochures. There is also a café here to revive yourself, which is fairly crucial when taking in the ancient sites.
🕐 09.30–18.30; tours 11.00–15.00 Sat. Admission charge

Foro Augusto (The Forum of Augustus) Just to the east of the Via dei Fori Imperiali is a round brick façade that houses the Order of Malta but was once part of the Forum of Augustus. The original staircase and platform can still be seen of what Augustus dedicated as the Temple of Mars, honouring the God of War after he had successfully avenged his uncle's assassins, Brutus and Cassius.

Foro Traiano (The Forum of Trajan) One of the most important areas of the Imperial Fora was the Forum of Trajan, a vast area dating from AD 107 that included shops, homes, churches and libraries. Sadly, very little remains today of what must have been a spectacular creation.

The main trading area was Trajan's Markets, not dissimilar to a modern shopping mall, but only a few columns now mark the spot. Also here was a wine and oil storage area, as well as a hall in which corn was rationed to the people when food was in short supply. Beneath the shops was once the Basilica Ulpia, but little now remains except for a few ruined columns and a paved area that indicates the position of the former nave. The new **Imperial Fora Museum** (☏ 06 820 59127), set in the main hall, houses 172 original marble fragments from the Fori Imperiali.

Also worth seeing is the impressive Trajan's Column, a 30 m (100 ft) high tribute to the Emperor's victory in the wars against Dacia (modern-day Romania), with carved reliefs documenting his achievements in exacting detail. The bronze statue on top of the column is of St Peter, placed here by Pope Sixtus V in the 16th century. ⓐ Trajan's Markets: Via IV Novembre ⏰ 09.00–18.00 Tues–Sun. Admission charge

Via dei Fori Imperiali The area now occupied by Via dei Fori Imperiali was once an atmospheric area of Roman and medieval alleyways starting from Piazza Venezia, until Mussolini decided to raze them in 1932 and replace them with this straight, broad street. While much of the original charm of the area may be gone (and with it, undoubtedly, some historic treasures), the street does now make all the ancient sights accessible in a more orderly fashion. The best time to visit is on Sundays, when the road from Piazza Venezia to Via Appia Antica is barred to traffic.

TAKING A BREAK

Enoteca Corsi £ ❶ A gem of a find between Piazza Venezia and the Pantheon. A highly traditional Roman *trattoria* and wine shop that serves a limited but delicious menu of whatever the owners happen to have cooked that morning. Very busy at lunchtime, but worth the wait. ⓐ Via del Gesù 87–88 ☏ 06 679 0821 ⏰ Lunch only; closed Sun 🚌 Bus: 23, 30, 46, 62, 63, 64, 70, 81, 87, 492, 628, 630, 780, 916; Tram: 8

Il Forno di Campo de' Fiori £ ❷ Great place for classic pizzas such as *pizza bianca* (drizzled with olive oil) and *pizza rossa* (with a tiny smear of tomato sauce) piping hot from the wood-fired oven. Has a deservedly loyal clientele. ➎ Campo de' Fiori 22 ☎ 06 688 01594 🕒 07.00–13.30 Mon–Sat, closed Sat evening in summer, Thur evening in winter ⓝ Bus: 30, 40, 46, 62, 64, 70, 81, 87, 116, 186, 204, 492, 628, 916

La Scaletta £ ❸ Centrally located *birreria* that's good for its reviving snacks, hot meals or just a drink between sights. ➎ Via della Maddalena 46–49 ☎ 06 679 2149 🕒 12.00–15.30, 18.00–00.30 ⓝ Bus: 62, 63, 81, 85, 95, 116, 117, 119, 160, 170, 204, 492, 628, 630, 850

AFTER DARK

Vecchia Roma £ ❹ A real find – the pizzas here are not your run-of-the-mill Margheritas, but employ real imagination in their toppings. ➎ Via Leonina 10 ☎ 06 474 5887 🕒 17.00–23.00 ⓝ Bus: 3, 8, 75, 85, 87, 117, 186; Metro: Cavour

Da Baffetto ££ ❺ A tiny neighbourhood favourite, famous for its enormous pizzas (you may want to share one between two), as well as for its *bruschette* with toppings such as white beans and fresh vegetables. Good value, with tables outside in summer, but do be prepared to queue, especially in the evening. ➎ Via del Governo Vecchio 114, off Piazza Pasquino ☎ 06 686 1617 🕒 19.00–00.00 ⓝ Bus: 30, 40, 46, 62, 64, 70, 81, 116, 492, 628

Giggetto al Portico D'Ottavia ££ ❻ In existence since 1923, three generations of the Ceccarelli family have owned this establishment.

● *Watch the professional pizza chefs throw dough at Da Baffetto*

It's the only place in Rome where you can get traditional Italian kosher food: try the *carciofi alla Giudea* (Jerusalem artichokes made the Jewish way) or the *baccalà* (salt cod). ⓐ Via del Portico D'Ottavia 21a–22 ⓣ 06 686 1105 ⓦ www.giggettoalporticodottavia.it

Glass Hostaria ££–£££ ❼ Cross the Ponte Sisto to Trastevere for excellent taster menus and creative dishes and desserts. Young chef Fabiana Cetorelli operates in an inviting minimalist setting, and this is a memorable gourmet dining experience. ⓐ Vicolo del Cinque 58 ⓣ 06 583 35903 ⓛ 20.00–23.30 Tues–Sun ⓦ www.glass-hostaria.com ⓝ Bus: H; Tram: 8

Vatican City

On the west bank of the Tiber lies the Vatican City State, the smallest independent state in the world, covering just over 40 hectares (100 acres). The state was established as an autonomous sovereignty in 1929 after agreement between the King of Italy and the Papacy acknowledged that the church could not be ruled under political regimes but needed to establish its own rules according to the Roman Catholic faith. Today, the Vatican is populated by fewer than 1,000 citizens and has its own militia, the Swiss Guards.

The area might be small in terms of world geography. However, it can take visitors several days to explore the entire area and only the very dedicated will have the stamina to do so.

The public entrance into Vatican City is through Bernini's glorious Piazza San Pietro (St Peter's Square), which offers a breathtaking introduction to the glories that are to come. Straight in front is the towering façade of St Peter's Basilica and the pillared colonnade decorated with statues of 140 saints. In front of this is an obelisk brought here from the ancient Egyptian city of Heliopolis and two fountains also placed here by Bernini.

❶ Proper dress is required for visiting the Vatican; this means long trousers for men, long trousers or knee-length skirts for women, covered shoulders (no sleeveless tops) and no bare feet. Unless you comply with these regulations you will not be allowed into the Vatican, St Peter's or any of the museums.

CULTURE

Basilica di San Pietro (St Peter's Basilica)
Arguably the most well known and recognisable church in the

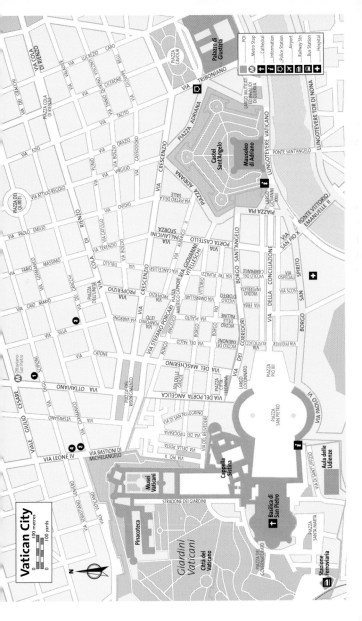

Christian world, and the seat of the Catholic church, St Peter's took more than 100 years to build, from 1506 to 1626. During that time some of the greatest names of the Renaissance contributed to its glorious whole. It takes its name from the supposed burial site of St Peter and a church had existed here since the fourth century AD, commissioned by the first Christian emperor, Constantine.

The first architect to lend his services to the new basilica was Bramante, who suggested the Greek Cross design topped by a central dome. After his death in 1514, the responsibility for completing the dome fell to Michelangelo, who worked on the project for nearly 20 years until his own death in 1564. The finished dome, probably the most famous in the world, was completed in 1590 by Giacomo della Porta, entirely to Michelangelo's original designs. The scale of the dome leaves no doubt as to how important this church was to be, at 120 m (394 ft) in height and 42 m (138 ft) in diameter. The sheer beauty of the structure went on to influence the design of many other landmark buildings around the world, among them London's St Paul's Cathedral, Les Invalides in Paris and the Capitol Building in Washington, DC.

Carlo Maderno was the final architect to work on the structure of the church from 1605 onwards, including the pillared façade and he turned it into a Latin plan that followed Constantine's original church.

❶ Proper dress is required to go inside the church; no shorts or bare shoulders are allowed.

Much of the quite stunning interior owes its baroque splendour to the sculptor Gian Lorenzo Bernini, who was a real superstar of that genre. A major flourish is the flamboyant *baldacchino* (canopy) that protects St Peter's tomb.

▶ *You'll find all manner of treasures inside St Peter's Basilica*

MUSEI VATICANI (VATICAN MUSEUMS)

The Vatican Museums are a vast collection of rooms and galleries to the east of St Peter's Basilica, housed in former Papal palaces largely dating from the 15th and 16th centuries.

The most famous area of the museums, and the one to which all visitors gravitate, is the Sistine Chapel (see page 104), but if you have the time and the stamina there are priceless collections to view in other parts of the complex.

The Pinacoteca is the main art gallery of the museums and features a stunning array of works, including some by Leonardo da Vinci. The Raphael Rooms conserve frescoes that were commissioned from the great artist by Pope Julius II. Other stunning 15th-century frescoes can be seen in the Borgia Apartment.

Classical statuary, largely Roman copies of Greek originals, can be seen in both the Pio-Clementine and Pio-Christian museums, including the famous *Apollo Belvedere*.

There are also museums dedicated to finds from ancient Egypt and from the Etruscan era.

In the middle of the museum complex are three courtyards: the Cortile del Belvedere at the southern end, the small Cortile della Biblioteca in the middle, created by the construction of

On the right side of the nave, behind protective glass since a crazed axe attack in 1972, is Michelangelo's beautiful Pietà. Completed when he was just 25, it clearly shows his genius in sculpting the human body. Further on, in the right transept is a sculpture of Pope Clement XIII by Canova, then a 13th-century bronze

the Vatican Library and Braccio Nuovo, and the northernmost of the three, Cortile della Pigna, named after the huge bronze *pigna* (pine cone) mounted in the niche at the end. If you are on a guided tour you will be stopped here to talk through the Sistine Chapel paintings before going in, as it is forbidden to speak inside.

The former main entrance to the museums was created by Pope Pius XI in 1932, and its huge bronze spiral staircase, in a double helix design, the work of Giuseppe Momo, made a fitting monumental prelude to the ticket offices above. On it are displayed the heraldic arms of all the Popes from 1447 to 1922 – Nicholas II to Pius XI's predecessor Benedict XV. Sadly, the museum entrance was recently updated and restructured so that you now enter through a door in the bastion wall to the left of Pius XI's entrance, through a large hall and a new marble staircase. An escalator carries you up to the museums.

It's not necessary to take a guided tour, although this will give you greater insight into the collections. If you prefer to be independent and selective, remember that you must follow the one-way system and that some collections can be closed or moved around with little notice. Refer to the website (ⓦ www.vatican.va) for up-to-date information.

of St Peter, said to be by Arnolfo di Cambio. Under Michelangelo's dome is the *baldacchino* (c. 1524), a 29 m high (96 ft) canopy made from the bronze stripped from the Pantheon roof.

A visit to the treasury is worthwhile to view a portion of the jewels that make up the riches of the Catholic church.

Another must-see is the tombs of the ancient and modern Popes at the Vatican Grottoes. Behind a wall of glass is the supposed tomb of St Peter. Leaving the grottoes, exit into a courtyard and the ticket office for the climb (or lift) up to Michelangelo's dome. Once you reach the top the views over Rome are stupendous.

ⓐ Piazza San Pietro ⓣ 06 698 81662 ⓦ www.vatican.va ⓛ Basilica: 07.00–19.00 Apr–Oct; 07.00–18.00 Nov– Mar; Grottoes: 08.00–17.00 Nov–Mar; Dome: 08.00–17.00 Oct–May; 08.00–18.00 Apr–Sept ⓝ Bus: 23, 40, 62, 64, 115, 116, 271, 280; Metro: Ottaviano then a long walk

ⓘ If you want to tour the *necropolis vaticana* (the area around St Peter's tomb), you must apply in advance at the Uficio Scavi through the arch to the left of the stairs up the Basilica (ⓣ 06 698 85318). You leave your name, number in your party and the dates you would like to visit and you will then be notified by telephone with the date, time and price of your tour.

There are 12 museums connected with the Vatican (see page 102), but the absolute unmissable is the Cappella Sistina (Sistine Chapel). Pope Julius II commanded the young artistic genius Michelangelo to decorate the ceilings of the Pope's Chapel with frescoes, a project that was to take four years of constant labour between 1508 and 1512. Michelangelo despised the project, not only for its difficulty, suspended from scaffolding, but because he was keen to devote his time to sculpture, but the final result was to prove to be his most famous work and one of the finest artworks in the world.

The most famous of some 33 ceiling panels are the *Creation of Adam* and the *Creation of Eve*, but there are many other panels that depict other parts of the Book of Genesis. On the altar wall is the *Last Judgement*, completed 20 years after the frescoes when

VATICAN PRACTICALITIES

The Vatican Museums and St Peter's Basilica are open to visitors (no shorts or bare shoulders for the Basilica), and it is also possible to visit the Vatican Gardens, though only on one guided tour a day (🕓 Mon & Tues, Thur–Sat, except religious holidays). It costs around €12, lasts approximately two hours and tickets must be bought several days ahead from the **Vatican Information Office** in Piazza San Pietro (🕿 06 698 84486 🌐 www.vatican.va). You pay when you pick up your tickets on the day of your tour.

You can attend a Papal audience, usually held on Wednesdays at 11.00 in the Audiences Room, but remember that these are not one-on-one affairs – dozens of other people will be there too. It's possible to get a ticket if you apply no more than a month and not less than two days in advance, by sending a fax with your name, home address, Rome address and your preferred date of audience to the **Prefettura della Casa Pontificia** (🕿 06 698 84857 📠 06 698 85863).

Finally, if you want to send a postcard with a Vatican postmark, there are Vatican post offices on the north side of Piazza San Pietro and inside the Vatican Museums.

Michelangelo was in his 60s. Other wall frescoes are by Renaissance painters such as Botticelli, Perugino, Pinturicchio and Ghirlandaio. ➌ Vatican City, Viale Vaticano 🕿 06 698 83860 🌐 www.vatican.va 🕓 08.30–18.00 (last admission 16.00) Mon–Sat; also 08.30–14.00 last Sun of each month 🚊 Tram: 19; Metro: Cipro–Musei Vaticani. Admission charge

RETAIL THERAPY

There are a few shops in Vatican City and in the museums. St Peter's Square is crammed with outdoor vendors selling souvenirs.

TAKING A BREAK

Non Solo Pizza £ ❶ The name means 'not just pizza' so expect other dishes and salads too. ⓐ Via degli Scipioni 95–97 ❶ 06 372 5820 🕒 08.30–22.00 Tues–Sun ⓝ Bus: 23, 32, 34, 40, 49, 62, 81, 280, 492, 590, 982; Tram: 19; Metro: A Ottaviano

AFTER DARK

Dal Toscano ££ ❷ Famous for its Tuscan T-bone steaks at honest prices. ⓐ Via Germanico 58–60 ❶ 06 397 25717 🕒 12.30–15.00, 20.00–23.00 Tues–Sun ⓝ Bus: 23, 32, 34, 40, 49, 62, 81, 280, 491, 590, 982; Tram: 19; Metro: Ottaviano–San Pietro

Ristorante Il Matriciano ££ ❸ Family restaurant conveniently located near St Peter's with regional Italian specialities. ⓐ Via dei Gracchi 55 ❶ 06 321 2327 🕒 12.30–15.00, 20.00–23.30 Thur–Tues, winter; 12.30–15.00, 20.00–23.30 Sun–Fri, summer ⓝ Metro: Ottaviano–San Pietro

Hostaria dei Bastioni £££ ❹ Fish is the speciality here. ⓐ Via Leone IV 29 ❶ 06 397 23034 🕒 12.00–15.00, 19.00–23.30 Mon–Sat (reservations recommended for Fri & Sat), closed mid-July–late Aug ⓝ Metro: Ottaviano

⊙ *The Villa d'Este in Tivoli is a spectacular sight*

OUT OF TOWN

Tivoli

Located 40 km (25 miles) from Rome, hill-top Tivoli, with its ideal position on the Aniene River, is both a proverbial and literal breath of fresh air from the noise and fumes of the capital. This was not something that was sniffed at even in ancient times, when the Romans used the area to escape the stifling heat of summer. During Renaissance times, too, some of the city's most prominent citizens built spectacular villas here. Today Tivoli largely makes its living from the quarrying and export of the local travertine rock, as any visitor will see if they drive the SS5 route from Rome to here.

The main attractions for visitors to Tivoli today are its three UNESCO World Heritage Sites: Hadrian's Villa Adriana and Villa d'Este. In order to take in everything you will need plenty of time, so either set out early on the day of your visit, or stay overnight in one of the small hotels.

Tourist Office Azienda Autonoma di Turismo ➌ Largo Garibaldi
🛈 0774 334 522 🕐 09.00–13.00, 15.00–17.00 Mon–Fri, 09.00–19.00 Sat

GETTING THERE

By rail
Local trains connect Rome's Tiburtina station with Tivoli with a journey time of about 30 minutes. There is a shuttle bus service from the station to the town centre and Villa d'Este. See **Trenitalia** (🛈 89 20 21 🌐 www.ferroviedellostato.it).

By road
COTRAL buses (🛈 800 150 008 🌐 www.cotralspa.it) leave Rome for Tivoli every 20 minutes from the terminal on the Ponte Mammolo

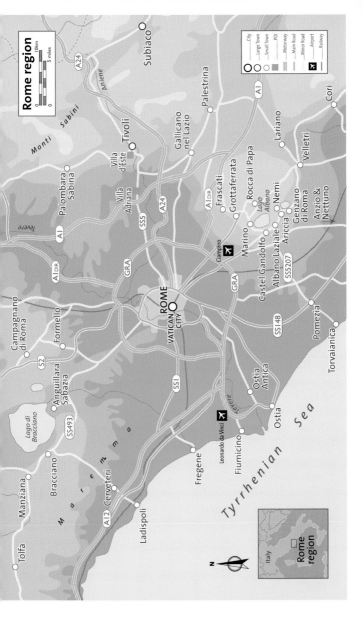

stop, on metro line B. The trip takes about an hour. There is a shuttle bus service from Tivoli's main square to Villa Adriana.

SIGHTS & ATTRACTIONS

Villa Adriana (Hadrian's Villa)

Tivoli's main attraction, just outside the town, is the Villa Adriana (Hadrian's Villa), built by the emperor between AD 118 and 134. Hadrian loved to experiment with architecture (much of the Pantheon can be attributed to his designer's eye) and his villa is no exception, with walkways, water features and colonnades.

Much of the site is now in ruins, but it still makes for an evocative and relaxing visit, strolling the ponds and gardens, and trying to recreate in one's mind what was once one of the most stunning villas of the imperial age. Sadly the main palace buildings are the least recognisable, but other areas of the complex clearly illustrate the influences Hadrian brought back with him from Greece and Egypt. The massive Pecile through which you enter, for example, is a reproduction of a building in Athens. One of the loveliest parts of the complex, the Canopus, is a copy of the sanctuary of Serapis near Alexandria, with its long strip of water decorated on either side by columns and statues.

Like so much of the area in and around Rome, the wealth of history means that archaeologists are constantly uncovering more and more treasures. A small museum near the Canopus gives some insight into the relics that have been excavated here and the ongoing work to discover more.

Among the other ruins that still evoke their original purpose are two bath complexes, a *cryptoporticus* (underground passageway) adorned with the autographs of visiting artists from the Renaissance and baroque periods, including Bernini, and the Teatro Maritimo

◆ *The Villa Adriana is an architectural beauty*

(Maritime Theatre). A circular brick wall here, 45 m (150 ft) in diameter, encloses a moat beyond which is an island of columns and a *domus* (little villa), complete with its own baths, bedrooms and gardens. The bridge across the moat today is made of cement, but the original would have been a wooden pathway that could be hauled up for extra privacy. It is the place to which it is believed that Hadrian retired at siesta time in order to be alone.

VILLA D'ESTE

Another important sight in Tivoli is the Villa d'Este, a lavish palace built over the ruins of a Benedictine monastery in 1550 for Cardinal Ippolito d'Este, son of Lucretia Borgia. The cardinal wanted a residence every bit as spectacular as Hadrian's had been – he got one

The brilliant frescoes by Correggio, Da Volterra and Perin Del Vaga in its seven rooms depicting scenes from the history of the d'Este family in Tivoli are certainly worth seeing if you're an art lover. But the real highlight, and what draws most visitors, is the gardens, which many consider to be the most attractive in Italy. Tiered and landscaped, and made up of manicured lawns and shrubbery, the grounds are dotted with some 51 fountains, including the Fontana del Bicchierone, designed by the great baroque sculptor Bernini, and a hydraulic fountain whose mechanism emulates the sound of music. If you were ever in doubt as to the extravagance of wealthy Renaissance families, the Villa d'Este should put you right. ⓐ Piazza Trento 1 ⓘ 0774 312 070 ⓦ www.villadestetivoli.info ⓛ 09.00–one hour before sunset Tues–Sun. Admission charge

Despite the grandeur and ambition of the project, Hadrian only enjoyed his retirement villa for three years before his death in 138. After the fall of the Roman Empire, it regularly fell into the hands of looters and treasure hunters, who sold their finds to museums all over the world. Marble and mosaic finds from here now make up a large proportion of the collections of Roman art at the Musei Capitoline (see page 62). ❸ Via di Villa Adriana ❶ 0774 530 203

⬥ Villa d'Este's water features rival any today

Ⓦ www.villa-adriana.net Ⓛ 09.00–one hour before sunset.
Admission charge

TAKING A BREAK

Adriano ££ Across from the entrance to Villa Adriano, the better-than-average menu here includes home-made pasta, and there's also a garden for al fresco dining. The Adriano's on-site inn also offers ten elegant but quite expensive guest rooms. Ⓐ Largo M Yourcenar 2 Ⓣ 0774 382 235 Ⓦ www.hoteladriano.it Ⓛ 12.30–16.00, 19.30–23.00

ACCOMMODATION

B&B Luigia £ A small, unpretentious bed and breakfast, with on-site restaurant, located 3 km (2 miles) from Tivoli centre. Ⓐ Via Villa Adriana 186 Ⓣ 0774 531 441, 339 429 1762

Hotel Le Rose £ Simple, clean rooms with full amenities, and restaurant offering typical Italian cooking. Near railway and bus stations. Ⓐ Via Tubertina 256 Ⓣ 0774 357 930 Ⓦ www.lerosehotel.it

Hotel Terme ££ Modern rooms with televisions and air conditioning, pool, restaurant and parking, 6 km (4 miles) from Tivoli historic centre. Ⓐ Piazza Bartolomeo della Queva 6 Ⓣ 0774 371 033 Ⓦ www.hoteltermetivoli.it

◉ *Hilltop Tivoli – a breath of fresh air*

Ostia & Ostia Antica

Visitors to the ruins of Ostia Antica need to make a few preparations to maximise their enjoyment of what will be a thrilling experience: the harbour area of Ancient Rome contains some archaeological features that are tremendously evocative of how vivid this part of the city must once have been. Comfortable walking shoes are imperative, and it's a good idea to avoid scheduling your exploration for the hottest part of the day. Whenever you come, do bring your own bottled water – to guard against both the heat and the exorbitant prices charged by local vendors!

GETTING THERE

By rail
Take Metro Line B from Stazione Termini to the Ostiense metro stop. Change here for the Lido train to Ostia Antica. Departures are every 30 minutes, and the trip takes 20 minutes.

By road
Follow Via del Mare southwest which leads directly from Rome to Ostia, with a journey time of around 40 minutes. Avoid driving on summer weekends when Romans head en masse to the beach.

By water
Two boat companies operate regular services to Ostia Antica. Both depart from Ponte Marconi (Marconi Bridge) in Rome. The trip down the Tiber takes 2 hours 15 minutes.
Battelli di Roma ❶ 06 977 45498 Ⓦ www.battellidiroma.it
🕒 Departures 10.00 summer; 09.30 winter (return trip from Ostia 14.00 summer; 13.30 winter)

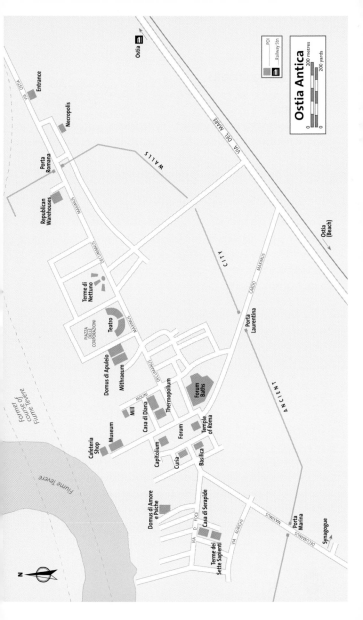

SIGHTS & ATTRACTIONS

Ostia Antica

Situated on the Tyrrhenian coast, Ostia Antica was a vital trading port in the days of the Roman Empire, and home to a motley crew of sailors and wealthy merchants. Much of the riches of the empire depended on the ability to import and export between the Mediterranean and North Africa, and the vast second-century *horrea* (warehouses) were built to house grain shipments. However, when the course of the River Tiber changed, the port became silted up and the once-prosperous city was abandoned to the elements. This may have affected the way of life in the early millennium, but the sand covering was a saving grace for 20th-century archaeologists engaged in the extensive Scavi di Ostia Antica (Ostia Antica excavations) that revealed the mysteries of this ancient area.

Before starting your explorations of the ruins take a look around the lovely medieval *borgo* (old town) and the impressive Castello delle Rovere, accessed via the footbridge from the train station. It was built by Pope Julius in 1483 when he was Cardinal of Ostia Antica. Inside are faded frescoes, reportedly completed by Baldassare Peruzzi, a student of Michelangelo.

The main street of Ostia Antica is the Decumanus Maximus, which leads past the Terme di Nettuno (Baths of Neptune), from which there is a good view of the polychrome mosaic pavements depicting Neptune and Amphitrite. Behind the baths was a fire department, which filtered water from the harbour whenever the vital warehouses were at risk. The commercial centre is known as Piazza delle Corporazioni where ground-floor shops and offices can still be identified by the mosaics depicting individual trades: grain merchant, ship-fitter, rope-maker and so forth. On one side of the

LIDO DI OSTIA

Romans are ever in search of places to escape from the summer heat and this coastal town was created in the 1930s for just that purpose. It is commonly referred to as Ostia Moderna (New Ostia) to differentiate it from the ruins of Ostia Antica, and is reached from Rome by the Via Cristoforo Colombo near the Baths of Caracalla.

However, not only is this stretch of beach heaving with crowds in summer, the water and the coast line leave a lot to be desired in terms of cleanliness. Far better options are at Torvaianica 11 km (7 miles) south of Ostia, which pays more attention to the state of the environment, as does the Castelporziano/Capocotta beach between Ostia and Torvaianica. In addition there's a nature reserve across the street from the beach, which means that your sunbathing scenery consists of sea on one side and sand dunes on the other.

On the Lido itself there are beach cafés and restaurants as well as a gay section, *Il Buco* (the hole), to which gays and lesbians flock from June to September, and a nudist section signposted *Oasi Naturista di Capocotta*. The nudist section of the beach has the best restaurants.

square, the beautiful *teatro* (theatre) was built by Agrippa, and restored by Rome city council in the 20th century so that it could continue to stage open-air performances.

Many of the former residences and temples can still be made out, despite their ruined status. The Domus di Apuleio (House of Apulius) was built in low-level Pompeian style with few windows;

🔺 *Imagine the hustle and bustle of Ostia Antica in Roman times*

the Casa di Diana (House of Diana) clearly shows several rooms surrounding a courtyard, as does the Domus di Amore e Psiche (House of Cupid and Psyche), which also has a well-preserved marbled floor. The Casa di Serapide (House of Serapis) is a second-century multilevel dwelling, while one street further along are insulae (apartment buildings) that provided housing for a large majority of Ostia's population.

One of the most fascinating remains, if only because it illustrates how little has changed between ancient and modern times, is the *thermopolium* (bar), a Roman café complete with seats outside and a fresco indicating the menu on offer.

North of the House of Diana is the museum, which houses numerous items excavated from the site, including frescoes that illustrate daily life in Ostia in ancient times, along with elegant sarcophagi and a statue of Mithras Slaying the Bull from one of Ostia's mithraea. West of the museum is the Forum where the city's most important temple (dedicated to Jupiter, Juno and Minerva), was located, as well as thermal baths, a basilica (which in Roman times was a secular hall of justice) and smaller temples. Continue on down the main street, and to the right you'll see some of the ancient warehouses that have been wonderfully preserved.

The Terme dei Sette Sapienti (Baths of the Seven Wise Men) are named after a collection of rather suggestive frescoes that were excavated from the site. The Porta Marina leads to what was once the seashore.

To the south of the port are the ruins of the synagogue, considered to be one of the oldest in the Western world.

ⓐ Viale dei Romagnoli 717 ⓣ 06 563 52830 ⓦ www.ostiaantica.net
ⓛ 08.30–one hour before sunset, Tues–Sun. Admission charge

TAKING A BREAK

The best seafood restaurants can be found on the Castelporziano/ Capocotta beach between Ostia and Torvaianica, particularly along the nudist section. The museum at the excavations has a cafeteria that serves breakfasts and light lunches.

Cipriani ££ A small atmospheric *trattoria*, located on a side street in the medieval old town. Hearty Italian food and reasonable prices. ⓐ Via del Forno 11 ❶ 06 563 59560 🕒 12.30–16.00, 19.30–23.00

ACCOMMODATION

Agli Scavi di Ostia Antica £ This small villa is only 100 m (330 ft) from the entrance to the excavations. All rooms have private baths and air conditioning, and breakfast is included. ⓐ Via della Stazione di Ostia Antica ❶ 06 565 7308 ⓔ sake@ostiaantica.net

Rome Country Residence ££ Modern accommodation with 21 self-catering apartments equipped with all amenities. ⓐ Largo Pasquale Testini 13 ❶ 06 563 52793 ⓦ www.romancountry.com

Ostia Antica Park Hotel ££–£££ Modern, conveniently situated 80-room hotel. Breakfast included. ⓐ Viale dei Romagnoli 1041a ❶ 06 565 2089 ⓦ www.ostiaanticaparkhotel.it

▶ *Modern yet charming Rome Country Residence*

Bracciano & Cerveteri

Lago di Bracciano (Lake Bracciano) is the closest of northern Lazio's lakes to the city, formed by an extinct volcanic crater. Along with the beaches around Ostia, it is a favourite summer escape for Romans, particularly avid anglers, and is only 30 minutes by train from the city. Even if you don't want to try your hand with rod and line yourself, the restaurants surrounding the lake offer excellent freshly caught catch of the day.

The town of Cerveteri is not much to look at, but the necropolis just outside the town provides the most accessible Etruscan ruins in the area. There has been a settlement here since the tenth century BC when it was an important trade centre.

GETTING THERE

By rail

Trains for Bracciano depart from Rome's San Pietro station, and the journey time is around 30 minutes. Take the train that goes in the direction of Viterbo.

By road

Cerveteri is 30 km (19 miles) northwest of Rome. The best way to reach the town is by bus, as the railway station is at Lapispoli, 7 km (4 miles) from the centre. Buses depart from Rome's Lepanto metro station, Line A, every 30 minutes, arriving at Cerveteri's Piazza Aldo Moro. The trip takes 1 hour 20 minutes.

○ *The town of Bracciano sits on the western shore of the lake*

OUT OF TOWN

SIGHTS & ATTRACTIONS

Bracciano

Lago di Bracciano's main settlement is the town of Bracciano on the western shore. Towering over it is the **Castello Orsini-Odescalchi** (ⓐ Piazza Mazzini 14 ❶ 06 998 04348), a late-15th-century castle. While the castle's outer walls are largely in ruins, the interior houses some historic suits of armour and frescoes, and the view from the ramparts is beautiful. It has recently acquired fame as the place where Tom Cruise married Katie Holmes.

The best beach for swimming is on Via Argenti to the south of the town. You can rent a boat to mess about on the water, then refresh yourself in the nearby *trattorie*.

Cerveteri

Cerveteri, the Roman Caere, was a large and financially profitable city during the Etruscan era, benefitting particularly from trading links with Greece. Its wealth derived largely from the mineral riches of the Tolfa hills to the northeast. At one time the town spread over 8 km (5 miles), 30 times its present size, controlling territory that stretched for 50 km (31 miles). The city, along with other Etruscan territories, went into decline around 351 BC when the Romans took control of much of the area.

CULTURE

Museo Nazionale Cerite

Many of Cerveteri's archaeological finds have been removed to larger museums around the world, but the 16th-century Castello Raspoli in the centre of the old town has four large rooms containing

⬥ Cerveteri was the once wealthy city of the Etruscan federation

⬧ *One of the streets of the necropolis*

some of the items that were excavated from the necropolis, including vases, sarcophagi, terracotta pots and other everyday objects from the Etruscan period. ⓐ Piazza Santa Maria Maggiore, Cerveteri ⓣ 06 994 1354 ⓛ 09.00–19.00 Tues–Sun

Necropolis & Museum

Most of Cerveteri dates from medieval times, but the necropolis, 1 km (½ mile) outside town, is a reminder that the area was important to the Etruscans. The ruins of this 'city of the dead' show the streets that meandered between tombs and burial chambers from the seventh to the first century BC. The male dead were buried in stone sarcophagi, accompanied by the cremated ashes of their slaves, while women were interred in separate burial chambers. Today you can see 12 tombs between the two roads that bisect the city. Among them are the Tomba Bella (Tombs of the Bas Reliefs), Tomba dei Letti Funebri (Tombs of the Funeral Beds), the Tomba degli Scudi e delle Sedie (Tombs of the Shields and Chairs), which consists of separate rooms linked by hallways, and the Tomba dei Rilievi (Tombs of the Reliefs) decorated with carvings.. ⓣ 06 994 0001 ⓛ 08.30–one hour before sunset Tues–Sun. Admission charge

TAKING A BREAK

Antica Locanda Le Cinestre Rustic chic with hearty food and attentive service. ⓐ Piazza Santa Maria 5, Cerveteri ⓣ 06 994 0672 ⓦ www.le-ginestre.it ⓛ 12.30–16.00, 19.30–23.00

The Castelli Romani & around

Beyond the suburbs of Rome the 13 towns that make up the Castelli Romani area (see map page 109) were the place of choice for summer villas during the Roman Empire as well as castle-building during the Middle Ages, when the surrounding hills, the Colli Albani, were the summer playground for the rich and powerful. The best towns to visit on a short trip from Rome are Frascati and Grottaferrata, east of Lago Albano to the Monte Cavo and Rocca di Papa, Castel Gandolfo, and west of Lago Albano to the town Albano Laziale. The area south of Lago Albano – the towns of Genzano di Roma, Nemi and Velletri – also makes a good visit. Wine-lovers in particular should sample the local grapes at the many wineries, but even if you're just after a day trip to escape the hectic lifestyle of the city the area is only 20 minutes' drive from Rome and makes for a refreshing break.

GETTING THERE

By rail

Anzio is easier to get to by public transport than southern Lazio's other coastal towns. Trains from Rome's Termini Station run directly to the town (and on to Nettuno) at hourly intervals throughout the day. The journey takes about an hour on the slow double-decker train, and is very cheap (about €3 each way). If the ticket office at Anzio is closed, you can buy tickets from the newsagent next door. Anzio's station (a charming modernist design) is fairly central. The centre of town and the port are a ten-minute walk downhill.

A small railway line runs from Rome's Termini Station into the Alban Hills. Some services stop at Frascati, others continue to Albano Laziale, via Marino and Castel Gandolfo. Services are infrequent,

⬥ *The Castel Gandolfo is the Pope's summer retreat*

however, so check the timetables in the station or at the tourist office. Tickets can be bought at any newsstand at Termini Station but you'd be advised to buy a return (*andata e ritorno*), as the provincial stations are often unstaffed. The rail journey is very scenic, passing Rome's aqueducts, vineyards and market gardens before skirting Lake Albano.

By road

COTRAL buses (❶ 800 150 008) leave Rome every 30 minutes from the terminus above the metro station Anagnina Line A.

Despite the scenic rail trip, without question the best way to see the Castelli Romani is by car. You will be able to see more, and travelling at your own pace will enable you to get to the heart of this interesting and appealing area.

Coming from the A1 highway Milan–Rome at the Fiano Romano junction, follow directions to Roma Nord. Once on the GRA, exit at the 21–22 Tuscolana Anagnina junction and follow the signs for the various towns in the region.

SIGHTS & ATTRACTIONS

Anzio & Nettuno

About 40 km (25 miles) south of Rome, Anzio is an attractive little town with a lively central piazza and a busy fishing harbour. Sadly, it is still best known for the battles it witnessed during World War II, and two military cemeteries bear testament to the British and American soldiers who bravely gave their lives during the 1944 landings. The Museo dello Sbarco di Anzio (Anzio Beachhead Museum), housed in a 17th-century villa (Villa Adele) near the station, commemorates soldiers of all nationalities who took part in the campaign.

Unpleasant history aside, today Anzio is a lovely coastal village with excellent seafood restaurants around the harbour. The beaches, too, are a welcome escape, but they are likely to be vastly overcrowded in the height of summer.

Nettuno, a couple of kilometres down the coast and walkable by the coast road, is popular with surfers. If you don't want to ride the waves, though, the old quarter has several *trattorie* facing onto the main piazza.

Anzio Tourist Office ⓐ Piazza Pia 19 ⓣ 06 984 5147 ⓛ 09.00–13.00, 15.30–18.00

Nettuno Tourist Office The tourist office is located on the harbour. ⓣ 06 980 3335

Castel Gandolfo & west of Lago Albano

Even the Pope feels the need to escape the beating summer sun and retreats, via the ancient Via Appia, to his summer residence Castel Gandolfo. Named after the castle owned by the powerful 12th-century Genoese Gandolfo family, the fortress towers 400 m (1,312 ft) above Lago Albano. Between July and September the Papal address every Sunday at midday moves from St Peter's Basilica in the Vatican to the balcony of this far cooler option.

From Castel Gandolfo a panoramic road leads to Albano Laziale, one of the nicest towns along the Via Appia. The town's Piazza Mazzina looks south to the Villa Communale park with the partial remains of a villa that once belonged to Pomeroy. Along the main street, Corso Mattrotti, the church of San Pietro was built over the foundations of the baths of a Roman garrison. Near the church of Santa Maria della Stella is a small museum housing an archaeological collection of Etruscan and Roman artefacts that were found in the town. On Via della Stella is the Tomb of Horatii and the Curiatii, with buildings

MONTE CAVO & ROCCA DI PAPA

On the eastern side of Lago Albano the Via dei Laghi leads to the summit of the 949 m (3,114 ft) high Monte Cavo, which was once home to a convent and a temple to Jupiter. From here there is a road to the highest of the hill-top towns, Rocca di Papa, which is worth the winding trip to see the attractive old quarter dating from the Middle Ages.

dating from Rome's republican era. Ⓦ www.museicivicialbano.it
🕐 Museo Civico 09.00–12.30 Mon–Sat, 09.00–12.00 Sun, 16.00–19.00 Wed & Thur. Admission charge

🔽 *A great town to visit is Grottaferrata*

THE CASTELLI ROMANI & AROUND

South of Lago Albano

Genzano, two km (one mile) further on from Albano Laziale, has a pleasant medieval centre built around the Piazza Frasconi. A road from here leads along to Lago Albano's crater and sweeps down to the shore through dense woods. Try to visit in June when the road down from the main square is covered in flowers to celebrate Corpus Domini.

A detour east will take you to Nemi. Built high above a tiny crater lake of the same name, the village itself is not really worthy of a visit but the lake shore is a wonderful spot for a picnic. Again, try to visit the area in June when on the first Sunday there is a strawberry festival in the town of Genzano to celebrate its most famous product.

On the northern side of the lake is a local museum, containing the remains of two pleasure boats said to have been built by that most infamous of emperors, Caligula. The boats, like the Empire, did

not survive intact and sank to the bottom of the lake, but they were raised in the 1930s under the orders of Mussolini – hence the typically Fascist-style buildings in which they are now housed. Unfortunately the boats were set on fire during the final days of the German Occupation, so they are little more than ruins today, but they still offer an insight into ancient ship-building skills. 🕐 Museum 09.00–18.00. Admission charge

Frascati & around

Frascati, 20 km (12 miles) from Rome, is one of the most beautiful as well as the most famous of the Castelli Romani towns. The majestic, privately owned, Villa Aldobrandini, built by Giacomo della Porta in 1598, dominates the town and the gardens, which offers wonderful views across the region all the way to Rome, are open to the public.

Frascati is best known for its production of the eponymous dry white wine, and many wineries in the region offers tours and tastings. Check at the tourist office for days and times. One of the most pleasant lunch options in the region is to pick up some cold meats and cheeses from the stands on Piazza dei Mercano and head for one of the many *cantine*, where you can bring your picnic offerings and enjoy a glass of wine served from gigantic wooden barrels.

Approximately 3 km (2 miles) from Frascati is the medieval town of Grottaferrata, also known for its wine production and for its 11th-century Abbey, surrounded by impregnable walls and a dry moat. In the grounds is the church of Santa Maria, whose gorgeous Byzantine interior is decorated with 13th-century mosaics. In the small chapel of St Nilo are 17th-century frescoes by Domenichino. There is also a small **museum** (🕐 06.00–12.30, 15.30–19.00, summer; 06.00–12.30, 15.30–sunset, winter) in the town which will appeal to art lovers with exhibits of classical and medieval sculpture.

⬥ *The majestic Villa Aldobrandini is the nexus of Frascati*

Frascati Tourist Office ⓐ Piazza Marconi ⓣ 06 942 0331
ⓛ 08.00–14.00, 16.00–19.00 Tues–Fri, 08.00–14.00 Sat

TAKING A BREAK

Antico Ristorante Pagnanelli £££ This elegant restaurant, overlooking
Lake Albano, has been in operation since 1882. Fish is a speciality,
as is the homemade ice cream. ⓐ Via A Gramsci 4, Castel Gandolfo
ⓣ 06 936 004 ⓛ 12.30–15.00, 19.30–23.00 Wed–Mon
ⓦ www.pagnanelli.it

ACCOMMODATION

Hotel Villa Maria Luigia £–££ A small, inexpensive hotel situated in
its own private park. All rooms have modern amenities, and breakfast
is included. ⓐ Via di Cisternole 204, Frascati ⓣ 06 946 4430
ⓦ www.villamarialuiga.it

Hotel Villa Mercede £–££ A convenient location, and some rooms
have views overlooking Rome. Continental breakfast included,
plus pool. ⓐ Via Tuscolana 20, Frascati ⓣ 06 942 4760
ⓦ www.villamercede.com

Hotel Castelvecchio ££ A luxury hotel, five minutes' walk
from Castel Gandolfo. There's a good on-site restaurant and a
swimming pool. ⓐ Viale Pio XI 23, Castel Gandolfo ⓣ 06 936 0308
ⓦ www.hotelcastelvecchio.com

ⓞ *Bracciano is a busy market town*

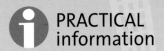

PRACTICAL
information

Directory

GETTING THERE

The best and least expensive means of travel to Rome is either by air or rail.

By air

Budget airlines have made it possible to fly direct from the UK to Rome into Ciampino from London Stansted, Glasgow Prestwick and East Midlands airports.

Fares depend on what season you choose to travel. The highest are at Easter, any time between June through to mid-August and Christmas through to New Year. Prices are considerably lower during the shoulder seasons of September to October, November to March and April to May. Weekend travel can add an extra ten per cent to the round-trip fare, not including taxes and airport charges.

Airlines in the UK, Ireland & Italy

Aer Lingus ❶ UK 0845 084 4444; Republic of Ireland 0818 365 0000 Ⓦ www.aerlingus.ie

Air Berlin ❶ UK 0870 738 8880 Ⓦ www.airberlin.com

Air Malta ❶ UK 0845 607 3710 Ⓦ www.airmalta.com

British Airways ❶ UK 0870 850 9850; Republic of Ireland 1 800 616 747 Ⓦ www.britishairways.com

easyJet ❶ UK 0871 750 0100 Ⓦ www.easyjet.com

Meridiana ❶ UK 0207 730 3454 Ⓦ www.meridiana.it

Ryanair ❶ UK 0871 246 0000; Republic of Ireland 0818 303 030 Ⓦ www.ryanair.com

TUIfly ❶ UK 0870 6060 519 Ⓦ www.tuifly.com

Volare ⓘ UK 0800 032 0992; outside UK +44 207 365 8235
Ⓦ www.volareweb.com

Airlines in the US & Canada
Air Canada ⓘ 1 888 247 2262 Ⓦ www.aircanada.ca
American Airlines ⓘ 1 800 433 7300 Ⓦ www.aa.com
British Airways US & Canada ⓘ 1 800 AIRWAYS
Ⓦ www.britishairways.com
Delta Airlines ⓘ 800 241 4141 Ⓦ www.delta.com
Iberia ⓘ 1 800 772 4642 Ⓦ www.iberia.com
KLM/Northwest ⓘ UK 0870 242 9242; US 1 800 447 4747
Ⓦ www.klm.com
Lufthansa ⓘ UK 0870 837 7747; US 1 800 645 3880;
Canada 1 800 563 5954 Ⓦ www.lufthansa.com
SAS Scandinavian Airlines ⓘ 1 800 221 2350 Ⓦ www.flysas.com

Booking flights online
The top four online booking sites are **Expedia** Ⓦ www.expedia.co.uk,
Orbitz Ⓦ www.orbitz.com, **Priceline** Ⓦ www.priceline.com and
Travelocity Ⓦ www.travelocity.com. Some others that offer
good deals and links to other discount websites are
European Travel Network at Ⓦ www.etn.nl/discount.htm or try
Ⓦ www.lastminute.com, www.hotwire.com, www.skyscanner.net
and www.travelsupermarket.com

Many people are aware that air travel emits CO_2, which
contributes to climate change. You may be interested in the
possibility of lessening the environmental impact of your flight
through the charity **Climate Care** (Ⓦ www.climatecare.org), which
offsets your CO_2 by funding environmental projects around the world.

By rail

The Europe-wide InterRail and Eurail passes give unlimited travel on the FS network.

Travelling by train to Rome is no less expensive than flying and the trip takes 16–18 hours from St Pancras International in London.

UK and Ireland
Eurail ⓦ www.eurail.com
Eurostar ⓣ 08705 186 186 ⓦ www.eurostar.com
InterRail ⓦ www.interrailnet.com
Rail Europe ⓣ 08708 30 20 08 ⓦ www.raileurope.co.uk

US and Canada
CIT Rail ⓣ US 1 800 223 7987 or 1 800 CIT TOUR, Canada 1 800 387 0711 ⓦ www.fs-on-line.com, www.cit-tours.com
Europrail International ⓣ Canada 1 888 667 9734 ⓦ www.europrail.net
Eurail ⓣ US 1 800 438 7245, Canada 1 800 361 7245 ⓦ www.raileurope.com/us

Australia and New Zealand
CIT World Travel ⓣ Australia 02 9267 1255 ⓦ www.cittravel.com.au
Rail Plus ⓣ Australia 1300 555 003 or 03 9642 8644, New Zealand 09 303 2484 ⓦ www.railplus.com.au
Trailfinders ⓣ Australia 1300 780 212 ⓦ www.trailfinders.com.au

The monthly *Thomas Cook European Rail Timetable* has up-to-date schedules for European international and national train services.
Thomas Cook European Rail Timetable ⓣ UK 01733 416477, USA 1 800 322 3834 ⓦ www.thomascookpublishing.com

By road

This is not the recommended mode of travel unless you have a phobia of flying or trains, as it takes a gruelling 24 hours or even longer.
National Express Eurolines ⓒ UK 08717 818181, Ireland 01 836 6111
ⓦ www.eurolines.co.uk

ENTRY FORMALITIES

British citizens need a valid passport to enter Italy. All other European Union (EU) citizens can enter the country by producing either a valid passport or a national identity card. All EU citizens may stay in the country for as long as they wish. Citizens of the United States, Canada, Australia and New Zealand need a valid passport, but are limited to stays of three months. All other nationals should consult the relevant embassies (see page 155) about requirements.

In terms of carriage of goods, there are almost no restrictions on what legal goods can be imported or exported to and from other EU countries, as long as you can prove that they are for your own use and not for resale. Large quantities of any item are likely to excite suspicion. To import tobacco or alcohol you must be over the age of 17.

For visitors from outside the EU, the restrictions on importing are as follows:

400 cigarettes; or 100 cigarillos; or 50 cigars; or 250 g of tobacco

60 cc of perfume

2 litres of still table wine

250 cc of eau de toilette

1 litre of spirits or strong liqueurs over 22 per cent volume; or 2 litres of fortified wine, sparkling wine or other liqueurs

£145-worth of all other goods including gifts and souvenirs.

MONEY

Italy's currency is the euro, and notes are issued in denominations of 5, 10, 20, 50, 100, 200 and 500 euros. Coins are issued in denominations of 1, 2, 5, 10, 20 and 50 cents, and 1 and 2 euros.

It is a good idea to have some cash to hand when you first arrive. There are ATMs and money exchange bureaux at the airports, and many scattered throughout Rome. The easiest way not to deal with exchange bureaux is by using your credit or debit card. Check with your bank to make sure that your personal identification number gives you access to cashpoint (ATM) machines abroad. The cards can be used at hotels, restaurants, some shops and for cash advances.

It's always a good idea to have some traveller's cheques on hand when you travel. Try to get them in different denominations, and keep the purchase agreement plus a record of the cheques' serial numbers in a different place from the actual cheques.

The most widely accepted traveller's cheques are **Thomas Cook** (Ⓦ www.thomascook.com) and **American Express** (Ⓦ www.americanexpress.com). If the cheques are lost or stolen, be sure to report it immediately to the issuing company. In most cases the cheques will be replaced within 24 hours.

On euro traveller's cheques you should not have to pay any commission when exchanging them for euros. For other currency cheques there is usually a commission charge of one per cent of the amount changed. Both Thomas Cook and American Express sell euro traveller's cheques.

HEALTH, SAFETY & CRIME

The European Health Insurance Card (EHIC) – formerly the E111 form – is valid for five years. The Australian Medicare system also has a reciprocal healthcare agreement.

◔ *Admire the fountains in the Piazza Navona*

Vaccinations are not required, and Italy does not present any serious health worries. The worst that could possibly happen to you is sunstroke from extreme heat in summer or an upset stomach.

An Italian *farmacia* (pharmacist) is very qualified to give medical advice on minor ailments and to dispense prescriptions. There are generally one or more pharmacies, open 24 hours on a rotation basis, in each district in Rome. You can find the contact information on any pharmacy door or in the local newspaper.

Gangs of *scippatori* (bag snatchers) strike in crowded streets, marketplaces and parks. Whether on foot or riding scooters, they act fast, disappearing before you have even had time to react. It is not only handbags they are after; they can whip wallets out of your pocket, tear off visible jewellery and cameras, and can even undo a watchstrap.

Do not flash around large sums of money, leave all jewellery at home, keep a firm grip on cameras, carry your handbag across your body and in front of you, put your wallet in your front pocket, or use a body wallet that you wear either around your waist or your neck under your clothing. Be vigilant when withdrawing money at cashpoints. Don't let anyone stand too close to you and try to distract you during a withdrawal. They may be trying to read your PIN number or use a skimmer to duplicate your card.

Avoid dark streets and alleys. If you are out late at night, swallow the expense and take a taxi back to your accommodation.

In the event of theft, report it to the police, which in Rome is principally between the *Vigli Urbani*, who are mainly concerned with traffic and parking tickets, or the *Polizia Statale*, the main crime-fighting force. There is also the *Carabinieri*, who deal with general crime. All three have offices in Termini, the central train station. The central police station is off Via Nazionale at Via San Vitale 15 (contactable via ☎ 06 4686). Prepare yourself for frustration.

OPENING HOURS

In general, opening hours are 16.00–19.30 for family-owned or food businesses and 10.00–13.00 and 16.00–19.30 for clothes and major chain or department stores. Most places are closed on Sundays and open at lunchtime or after on Mondays (many shops close on Saturday afternoons and Monday mornings). The big department stores, fashion-chain stores and many of the shops in and around Via del Corso, Via del Tritone, Piazza di Spagna and Via Nazionale stay open through lunch and do reduced hours on Sundays.

TOILETS

Train and bus stations are the best options, but facilities have improved around tourist sites in recent years. Most cafés and restaurants reserve use of facilities for patrons only. In some cases an attendant doles out *carta* (toilet paper) and expects a small tip. Toilets run the gamut from clean and modern to a hole in the floor. Have packets of sanitary wipes with you at all times.

CHILDREN

As elsewhere in family-orientated Italy, children are readily accepted in Rome. Indeed the city has gone to some considerable lengths over recent years to provide interesting attractions for the odd child who may not be a budding ancient historian: while sightseeing may bore very young children, you can keep them amused with plenty of alternative entertainments. The zoo at **Bioparco** at Villa Borghese (ⓔ Via del Giordino Zoologico, Ville Borghese 🛈 06 360 8211 Ⓦ www.bioparco.it) is a real child-pleaser. Indoor activities include **Time Elevator** (ⓔ Via dei Santissimi Apostoli 20 🛈 06 977 46243 Ⓦ www.timeelevator.it), an amazing experience where flight simulator seats and headphones give little ones (and their parents) a virtual tour of 3,000 years of Roman history. Then there's **Explora: Museo dei Bambini di Roma** (ⓐ Via Flaminia 82 ⓘ 06 361 3776 ⓦ www.mdbr.it), where children are encouraged to become aware of their place in the world – don't worry: it's loads of fun and nowhere near as earnest as it sounds. At the weekend the children can be entertained by an Italian puppet show on the Janiculum Hill. In Piazza Scanderbeg, close to the Trevi Fountain, is the **Museo Nazionale Delle Paste Alimentari** (ⓘ 06 699 1120 ⓦ www.pastainmuseum.it), where you can learn all about the history of the famous Italian pasta. A quick look around this establishment will soon have the whole family drooling. Bowling, ice skating, indoor rock-climbing and roller-skating are all popular in Rome.

As far as food goes, Rome offers meals that generally appeal to kids, such as *gelato* (ice cream), pizza and spaghetti, and most restaurants will serve half portions on request.

One of the major hazards when travelling with children in summer is the heat and sun. Make sure you bring plenty of high-factor sunscreen, as it is difficult to find in Rome, it being thought somewhat wimpish here not to be prepared to roast oneself or one's offspring alive for the sake of a nice tan. Never fear, though: hats are plentiful in local markets. If you do have little ones in tow, try to take advantage of mornings and evenings for travelling and sightseeing, and use siesta time to allow them to recover sapped energy (you'll be grateful for some feet-up time yourself). For minor indispositions, there are pharmacies all over the city, for which see the Health section of this guide (see page 144).

Supermarkets are also plentiful throughout the city and well stocked with nappies and baby food.

COMMUNICATIONS

Internet

There is good Wi-Fi connection in Rome, particularly in Villa Borghese. Internet terminals are easy to find, too. Hourly rates are €4–€6. Make sure you have ID to hand, as it is now required before using the internet in public internet cafés due to new anti-terrorist legislation.

Easy Internet Café @ Piazza Barberini 2 ☎ 06 429 03388 ⏱ 08.00–02.00

Museo del Corso @ Via del Corso 320 ☎ 06 678 6209 ⏱ 10.00–20.00 Tues–Fri, 10.00–22.00 Sat, 10.00–20.00 Sun

Phone

Telecom Italia runs the public phones in Rome. Instructions in English are usually posted in each phonebox. Coin-operated telephones are

TELEPHONING ITALY

From the UK, Ireland and New Zealand dial the access code 00 (011 from the USA and Canada, or 0011 from Australia), followed by the code for Italy (39), then the local number (including the 06 code).

TELEPHONING ABROAD

UK and Northern Ireland international access code 0044 + area code

Republic of Ireland international access code 00353 + area code

US & Canada international access code 001 + area code

Australia international access code 0061 + area code

New Zealand international access code 0064 + area code

almost extinct in Rome. It is best to purchase a *carta* or *scheda telefonica* (telephone card), available at *tabacchi* and newsstands for €2.50, €5 or €7.75. The perforated corners of these cards must be torn off before they can be used. The telephone code for Rome is 06, which must be dialled before any Roman number, even if calling in Rome. Numbers with 800 are free, and dialling 170 gets you an English-speaking operator. Dial 176 for international directory enquiries. The phone tariffs are very expensive, but there is a reduced rate for off-peak calls (weekdays 18.30–08.00, weekends 13.00 Sat–08.00 Mon for national calls, 22.00–08.00 Mon–Sat and all day Sun for international calls).

Calls to abroad can be made from most public phones with an international phone card, on sale at main post offices. The most common cards are the Columbus card for calls to Western Europe, and North America and the standard *Scheda Telefonica Internazionale* for the rest of the world. For a less expensive option at peak calling times, there is the Europa Card for calls to Europe, USA and Canada only. This card is not inserted into the phone. Instead a central number is dialled, followed by a PIN code which can be found on the reverse side of the card. You can also use your telephone charge card from your home telephone company. Using a PIN, calls can be made from most hotel, public and private phones with charges being put on your account. International reverse or collect calls can be made by dialling 170 and following the instructions.

In Italy mobile phones work on the GSM European standard. Before you leave home make sure you have made the necessary roaming arrangements with your company and find out what you will be charged for making and receiving calls. UK, New Zealand and Australian mobile phones will work in Italy, but US and Canadian cell phones may not. If you plan to stay for an extended period, or if you travel to Italy often, it may be worth purchasing an Italian SIM card (TIM or Vodafone mobile phone stores are two of the chain outlets that supply them). SIM cards normally cost between €5 and €10 and you'll need to show your passport when you make your purchase.

Post

The **main post office** in Rome (08.30–18.30 Mon–Fri, 08.30–13.00 Sat) is on Piazza San Silvestro. Other post offices open 08.30–14.00 Mon–Fri, 08.30–13.00 Sat. *Francoboli* (stamps) can be purchased in

 Blue post box in the Vatican City

tabacchi. Rome's postal system is the slowest in Europe, so if your letter or package is urgent it's best to send it by *posta prioritaria* (priority post). The rates vary according to weight and destination.

Central Post Offices

- Via Terme di Diocleziano 30 (Piazza Repubblica)
- Via Arenula 4 (Largo di Torre Argentina)
- Via Milano 10 (Via Nazionale)

ELECTRICITY

Electricity in Rome is 220 volts. Adaptors in Rome can be expensive, so it's best to try and bring one with you.

TRAVELLERS WITH DISABILITIES

Rome is not yet fully equipped for those with disabilities. The **Consorzio Cooperative Integrate** (COIN, Via Enrico Giglioli 54a 06 232 67504, free in Italy 800 271 027 www.coinsociale.it/tourism) publishes information regarding accessibility at Rome's major tourist attractions, accommodation and restaurants on its website, its 24-hour English-speaking phone line and in its free guide, *Roma Accessible*.

TOURIST INFORMATION

Tourist information booths are located in the arrivals section of Fiumicino airport, and at platform 2 at Termini Station. The main tourist office is a ten-minute walk from Termini, and has a wider selection of free maps, brochures and general information about the city sights. All have English-speaking staff members. Information kiosks are sprinkled throughout the city at visible locations. They are generally open 09.00–18.00. The Tourist Board's website is www.romaturismo.com

Tourist Board kiosk locations

Fiumicino 🕿 06 659 56074 🕒 08.15–19.00

Termini Station 🕿 06 489 0630 🕒 08.00–21.00

Piazza di Spagna Largo Goldoni 🕿 06 681 36061

San Giovanni Piazza San Giovanni in Laterno 🕿 06 772 03535

Via Nazionale Palazzo delle Esposizioni 🕿 06 688 09240

Piazza Navona Piazza delle Cinque Lune 🕿 06 688 09240

Castel Sant'Angelo Piazza Pia 🕿 06 688 09707

Fori Imperiali Piazza del Tempio della Pace 🕿 06 699 24307

Trastevere Piazza Sonnino 🕿 06 588 33457

The friendly, English-speaking staff at **Enjoy Rome** (🖂 Via Marghera 8a 🕿 06 445 1843 🕅 www.enjoyrome.com) offer a free room-finding service, tours and shuttle buses to the airport. They also provide maps and brochures, and advise where to eat, drink and party.

If all else fails, the city runs a hotline that gives information in many languages on the important things to see and do in Rome. 🕿 06 06 06 🕒 16.00–19.00 Mon–Sat

Other informational websites:

🕅 www.romeguide.it

🕅 www.capitolium.org

🕅 www.catacombe.roma.it

🕅 www.vatican.va

🕅 www.venere.it

BACKGROUND READING

I, Claudius and *Claudius the God* by Robert Graves. The most evocative of the novels about the characters who shaped imperial Rome.
Rome: The Biography of a City by Christopher Hibbert. A compelling account of the city's development.

Emergencies

EMERGENCY NUMBERS

Police ❶ 113, **Carabinieri** ❶ 112, **Fire** ❶ 115, **Ambulance** ❶ 118

MEDICAL SERVICES

Consult the yellow pages under *medico*. If you need urgent medical care go to the *pronto soccorso* (casualty department). All the hospitals listed below offer 24-hour casualty services.

Ospedale Fatebenefratelli ⓐ Isola Tiberina, Ghetto ❶ 06 68 371 ⓝ Bus: H, 23, 63, 280, 630, 780; Tram: 8

Ospedale Pediatrico Bambino Gesù (Children's Hospital) ⓐ Piazza Sant'Onofrio 4, Gianicolo ❶ 06 68 591 ⓝ Bus: 115, 870

Ospedale San Camillo-Forlanini ⓐ Via Portuense 332, Suburbs; west ❶ 06 55 551/06 58 701 ⓝ Bus: H, 228, 710, 719, 773, 774, 786, 791; Tram: 8

Ospedale San Giacomo ⓐ Via Canova 28, Tridente ❶ 06 36 261/06 322 7069 ⓝ Bus: 117, 119, 590; Metro: Spagna

Ospedale San Giovanni ⓐ Via dell'Amba Aradam 8, San Giovanni ❶ 06 77 051 ⓝ Bus: 81, 117, 650, 673, 714; Metro: San Giovanni

Policlinico Umberto I ⓐ Viale Policlinico 155, Suburbs; north ❶ 06 49 971 ⓝ Bus: 61, 310, 490, 491, 495, 649; Tram: 3, 19; Metro: Policlinico

Pharmacies

Farmacie (pharmacies) are identified by a green cross in the window or above the door. Along with dispensing prescriptions, Italian pharmacists are well qualified to give informal medical advice on minor ailments. Make sure you know the generic as well as the brand name of your regular medicines, as they may be sold under a different name in Italy.

EMERGENCY PHRASES

Help!	Fire!	Stop!
Aiuto!	Fuoco!	Fermi!
Ahyootoh!	*Fwohkoh!*	*Fehrmee!*

Call an ambulance/a doctor/the police/the fire service!
Chiami un'ambulanza/un medico/la polizia/i pompieri!
Kyahmee oon ahmboolahntsa/oon mehdeecoh/
lah pohleetseeyah/ee pohmpyehree!

Normal opening hours for pharmacies are: 08.30–13.30, 16.30–20.00 Mon–Fri. Outside these hours a duty rota system operates. A list by the door of any pharmacy and in local newspapers indicates the nearest one open at any time.

Farmacia della Stazione 🅰 Piazza dei Cinquecento 49–51, Esqualino
🛈 06 488 0019 🕘 08.00–18.00 Mon–Fri, 08.30–13.00 Sat Ⓝ Bus: C, H, 16, 36, 38, 40; Tram: 5, 14; Metro: Termini

Piram 🅰 Via Nazionale 228, Esqualino 🛈 06 488 0754 🕘 24 hours Ⓝ Bus: H, 40; Metro: Repubblica

EMBASSIES & CONSULATES
Australia 🅰 Corso Trieste 25 🛈 06 85 27 21, toll free 🛈 800 877 790
Canada 🅰 Via Zara 30 🛈 06 44 59 81
Republic of Ireland 🅰 Piazza Campitelli 3 🛈 06 697 9121
New Zealand 🅰 Via Zara 28 🛈 06 441 7171
UK 🅰 Via XX Settembre 80a 🛈 06 422 00001
USA 🅰 Via Veneto 119a 🛈 06 46 741

INDEX

WHAT'S IN YOUR GUIDEBOOK?

Independent authors Impartial up-to-date information from our travel experts who meticulously source local knowledge.

Experience Thomas Cook's 165 years in the travel industry and guidebook publishing enriches every word with expertise you can trust.

Travel know-how Thomas Cook has thousands of staff working around the globe, all living and breathing travel.

Editors Travel-publishing professionals, pulling everything together to craft a perfect blend of words, pictures, maps and design.

You, the traveller We deliver a practical, no-nonsense approach to information, geared to how you really use it.

SPOTTED YOUR NEXT CITY BREAK?

...then these lightweight CitySpots pocket guides will have you in the know in no time, wherever you're heading.

Covering over 90 cities worldwide, they're packed with detail on the most important urban attractions from shopping and sights to non-stop nightlife; knocking spots off chunkier, clunkier versions.

Aarhus
Amsterdam
Antwerp
Athens
Bangkok
Barcelona
Belfast
Belgrade
Berlin
Biarritz
Bilbao
Bologna
Bordeaux
Bratislava
Bruges
Brussels
Bucharest
Budapest
Cairo
Cape Town
Cardiff
Cologne
Copenhagen
Cork
Dubai
Dublin
Dubrovnik
Düsseldorf
Edinburgh
Fez
Florence
Frankfurt

Gdansk
Geneva
Genoa
Glasgow
Gothenburg
Granada
Hamburg
Hanover
Helsinki
Hong Kong
Istanbul
Kiev
Krakow
Kuala Lumpur
Leipzig
Lille
Lisbon
Liverpool
Ljubljana
London
Los Angeles
Lyon
Madrid
Marrakech
Marseilles
Milan
Monte Carlo
Moscow
Munich
Naples
New York City
Nice

Oslo
Palermo
Palma
Paris
Pisa
Prague
Porto
Reykjavik
Riga
Rome
Rotterdam
Salzburg
Sarajevo
Seville
Singapore
Sofia
Stockholm
Strasbourg
St Petersburg
Tallinn
Tirana
Tokyo
Toulouse
Turin
Valencia
Venice
Verona
Vienna
Vilnius
Warsaw
Zagreb
Zurich

Available from all good bookshops, your local Thomas Cook travel store or browse and buy online at www.thomascookpublishing.com

Thomas Cook Publishing

ACKNOWLEDGEMENTS & FEEDBACK

Editorial/project management: Lisa Plumridge
Copy editor: Paul Hines
Layout/DTP: Alison Rayner

The publishers would like to thank the following individuals and organisations for supplying their copyright photographs for this book: Alamy Ltd, page 114; Martin Belam, page 33; Carlos Fernández, page 97; Pictures Colour Library, pages 7, 26–7 & 101; Rome Country Residence, page 123; Kim S, page 151; Jon Smith, page 91; World Pictures/ Photoshot, pages 25, 31 & 75; Christopher Holt, all others.

Send your thoughts to
books@thomascook.com

- Found a great bar, club, shop or must-see sight that we don't feature?
- Like to tip us off about any information that needs a little updating?
- Want to tell us what you love about this handy little guidebook and more importantly how we can make it even handier?

Then here's your chance to tell all! Send us ideas, discoveries and recommendations today and then look out for your valuable input in the next edition of this title.

Email the above address (stating the title) or write to: CitySpots Series Editor, Thomas Cook Publishing, PO Box 227, Coningsby Road, Peterborough PE3 8SB, UK.